ONLINE DISTANCE EDUCATION

Online Distance Education

By

Marcelo C. Borba
Graduate Program of Mathematics Education, UNESP, Ria Claro, Brasil

Ana Paula dos Santos Malheiros
Federal University of Itajubá/GPIMEM, UNESP

and

Rúbia Barcelos Amaral Zulatto
State University of Campinas/GPIMEM, UNESP

SENSE PUBLISHERS
ROTTERDAM / BOSTON / TAIPEI

A C.I.P. record for this book is available from the Library of Congress.

ISBN 978-94-6091-291-7 (paperback)
ISBN 978-94-6091-292-4 (hardback)
ISBN 978-94-6091-293-1 (e-book)

Published by: Sense Publishers,
P.O. Box 21858, 3001 AW Rotterdam, The Netherlands
http://www.sensepublishers.com

This book was originally published in Portuguese under the title Educação a Distância online.
Copyright © Autentica editoria, 2001, covering material copyrighted by the Licenser.

Printed on acid-free paper

CONTENTS

ACKNOWLEDGEMENTS

We would like to thank all the teachers who participated in our various online distance education experiences and also all the members of our research group, GPIMEM who, since 1999, have helped us think about issues related to online distance education and put them into practice.   Although the contents of this book are entirely the responsibility of the authors, we would especially like to thank the following people for their criticisms and suggestions: Marcus Vinicius Maltempi, Mónica Villarreal, Nilza Bertoni, Ricardo Scucuglia, Sandra Malta Barbosa, Silvana Cláudia Santos, and Telma Gracias.

We would also like to thank the São Paulo State Research Foundation (FAPESP), the National Council for Scientific and Technological Development of Brazil (CNPq), Coordination for the Improvement of Higher Education Personnel of Brazil (CAPES) the Social Science and Humanities Research Council from Canada (SSHRCC), and the Bradesco Foundation, Brazil, for their direct or indirect support of research presented here.

Note from the Coordinator of the collection of books entitled Tendências em Educação Matemática (Trends in Mathematics Education):

This book is part of a collection of books called Trends in Mathematics Education. This collection began being published in 2001 and currently has 21 titles published by more than 30 different authors. It is designed to present research to a broader audience that extends beyond academia. The books have been widely used in graduate courses, research groups and in some undergraduate classes.   About 60,000 copies of the Portuguese edition have been sold. Some titles have been translated into Spanish and English.

Marcelo C. Borba

ACKNOWLEDGMENT TO THE TRANSLATOR

We would like to thank Anne W. Kepple who is responsible for the translation from Portuguese into English and who, in the process, helped to clarify some ideas with the participation of the authors.

Marcelo C. Borba, Ana Paula Malheiros, Rubia Amaral Zulatto

INTRODUCTION

Distance education, the Internet, and "downloading files" are expressions that have invaded our lives in recent years. For some, distance education is seen as something pernicious that should be banned to avoid affecting the quality of teaching. For others, however, it may be seen as a salvation or even a way to finally democratize student access to public universities. In this book, we attempt to escape this dualistic trap and present examples and research results of online distance education in action.

Online distance education can be understood as an educational modality that mainly takes place mediated by interactions via the Internet and associated technologies. Courses where the interaction occurs using interfaces such as chat rooms, videoconferences, forums, etc., are included in this modality. We will thus discuss how this form of education takes on its own shape and, in particular, how it molds mathematics education. We present accounts of what can be called online mathematics education. Using specific examples to illustrate, we will show how mathematics can be transformed when working with it in virtual environments.

Although the authors are all mathematics education researchers, and the large majority of examples are taken from courses for teachers in which the focus is mathematics or mathematics education, the reader will observe that the discussion can be adapted, in a "situated" manner, to other fields of knowledge.

We believe that education in virtual environments shapes the participation of students and teachers in a way that is analogous to how the classroom shapes this participation. Like Castells (2003), we see the Internet as being impregnated with social relations, not only with respect to the interactions among the humans who use it, but in the very way the Internet has distributed itself. It is no coincidence that broad-band Internet has arrived forcefully in economic centers while often failing to reach the pockets of the "Fourth World" in the poorer neighborhoods of large and medium-sized cities, as well as many rural areas where purchasing power and the "logic" of the market do not justify the installation of fiber optic cables.

The implementation of public policies that make Online Distance Education viable is fundamental to fill the immense gaps left by the (lack of) logic of the market. In this sense, tax exemptions for the purchase of computers are welcome, but the money from the Fund for the Universalization of Telecommunications Services (FUST)[1] should truly be put to use to create fiber optic networks dedicated to education, connecting schools and universities in the country.

Years ago, Borba and Penteado (2001) proposed that these funds be used to democratize Internet access. Its growth in education and for other ends indicates that we will soon be facing bottlenecks in access. A network for Internet only needs to be created with FUST funds, paid for by everyone who uses the telephone, as well as state and municipal governments. It is also necessary to criticize the so-called "right of passage", according to which companies responsible for managing the highways do not allow fibers purchased with public funds to pass by them. When more highways are privatized, it is fundamental, in the transportation sector, that the "right of passage" remain with the government so that companies do not charge exorbitant fees for the right, which should belong to everyone, to have access to the Internet.

Access to computer technology in general, and the Internet in particular, has become as important as guaranteeing that every child have paper, pencil, and books. Castells has proposed that the division between the First, Second, and Third World will be replace by another that creates the "Fourth World" in all regions of the planet. The immense accumulation of capital by some companies, and the lack of access to the Internet and to the wealth in general, which still persists, are only some of the ingredients of the "civil war" that is taking over so many Brazilian cities.

We are not proposing that Internet access will resolve the problems of inequality that have accumulated over the centuries – or decades, depending on how you look at it – in countries like Brazil, but rather understanding that it is analogous to what access to school represented in the past, and still represents today if you consider access to good schools.

However, access alone is not enough, unless we also understand how educational processes take place when the Internet becomes more than a mere supporting actor. Thus, we need to understand how to deal with it in an educational context. For example, it is necessary to recognize that interactions such as the multi-logue, proposed by Borba and Penteado (2001) and Gracias (2003), change the "etiquette" with respect to what is seen as correct in the interaction between teachers and students in a virtual classroom based on chat, since many people can express themselves simultaneously, in this case. These ideas, based on initial reflections on our experiences and research in online distance education, gather strength in this book as we analyze how written text, which characterizes chat, modifies the mathematics produced by participants in distance courses who use this interface as their main protagonist. Is it possible that it also modifies the geography, physics, biology, and arts learned by students, among other fields of knowledge?

The answer to this question lies beyond this book. On the other hand, we will show data and analyses regarding how those who engage in new forms of communication are experiencing continuing teacher education. We will show how distance courses can point to paths that approximate the daily practice of teachers in the classroom, as well as reflection on this practice, through the discussion of problems proposed to or by the teachers in courses that value the voices of those engaged in practice.

Of course there are different models of practice in virtual environments. The Internet is a symbol of diversity, and almost anything can be found there, including attempts to reproduce activities in this environment that are similar to those developed in traditional educational environments. Thus, just as there are those who "copy" the book onto the blackboard, there are those who see online distance education as merely "downloading files" from a web page. In this type of model, interaction with the teacher is not given priority, except in the form of prepared questions and answers stored in a data base of Frequently Asked Questions (FAQs). This main attraction of this model is the cost, but rarely does it adapt to learning in mathematics or other fields in which discussion is essential, although it is certainly possible to list the necessary steps to build an apiary, for example. Collaboration also stands out as a fundamental element of online distance education, to the degree to which we believe that learning is multidirectional, and not only from teacher to student, or student to student.

This book will thus address the discussion on online distance education, teacher education, and how the mathematics is transformed with the Internet, based on examples that illustrate the possibilities of different course models. Furthermore, we will attempt to give the reader the sensation of experiencing one of the various distance courses in which we have participated, or a virtual community that does not have the structure of a course. And if the reader has not yet participated in any of these possibilities, we believe that the book may help, but not substitute, the experience of participating in a discussion list, a course, or a virtual community constituted by a specific interest.

CHAPTER I

SOME ELEMENTS OF
ONLINE DISTANCE EDUCATION

As we reflected on online distance education in our research group, GPIMEM[1], certain questions emerged: "How does the teaching-learning process take place? What is the teacher's role in this new educational modality? How do different interfaces change the interactions among the participants?" These questions will be answered throughout this book, but we believe it is important to first present a brief historical retrospective on distance education in Brazil as well as some of the perspectives of those who, like ourselves, have been conducting research in this area.

We base our classification on that elaborated by Vianney et al. (2003) who carried out a longitudinal study of distance education in Brazil in which they identified three generations. The first emerged in 1904 with correspondence teaching, which emphasized professional education in technical fields, such as carpentry, trading, and others.

The second generation of distance education was defined by the emergence of high school equivalency courses for adults in the 1970s and 1980s which were usually carried out via satellite while students received printed material to study. Among the communications resources used were radio, television, audio tapes, and even videotapes on occasion.

In 1996, following two years of expansion of the Internet into the university environment, the first official legislation on distance education at the university level was passed. This expansion marked the beginning of the third generation of distance education, "which has been structuring itself based on advanced technology" (TORRES, 2004, p.31).

This generation of distance education has gained strength with the legislation. Fragale Filho (2003, p.13) explains:

> Viewed with mistrust, treated as a supplementary or complementary form of face-to-face teaching, it was practically ignored in legislative concerns related to regulation of education in Brazil. However, with the emergence of new technologies, the barriers were broken, making its spread possible, and leading to an unprecedented increase in demand and the introduction of its regulation into the legislative agenda.

Thus, addressing issues involving regulation, such as the distinction between distance and face-to-face education and the procedures needed to define and evaluate practices, became a challenge for educational policymakers "when they find themselves compelled to elaborate, approve, and implement legislative proposals for the sector" (FRAGALE FILHO, 2003, p.13).

Law No. 9.394, from December 20, 1996 (LDB – Basic Directives for Education in Brazil), presented quantitative and qualitative goals to be achieved in the sphere of distance education, no longer treating it as an experimental project (LOBO, 2000). Of the few articles that referred to distance education, paragraph 4 of article 80 assured that

> [...] distance education will enjoy differential treatment which will include: I) reduced transmission costs in commercial radio-dissemination, sound and image channels; II) concession of channels with exclusively educational purposes; III) reservation of a minimum time, without charge to the government, by the owners of commercial networks.

This article also states that distance education can only be offered by institutions credentialed by the Federal Government, whose responsibility it is to regulate the necessary requisites for examinations and diplomas. Thus, until regulation of these aspects had been achieved, the other regulations remained ineffective (LOBO, 2000).

Decree 2.494, on February 10, 1998, advanced a bit further, regulating article 80 of the LDB and defining distance education as

> [...] a form of teaching that enables self-learning, mediated by systematically organized didactic materials presented in different informational supports, used alone or in combination, and transmitted via diverse means of communication.

What one notes, as Fragale Filho (2003) pointed out, was that, in fact, article 80 of the LDB did not clearly explain the legislative concept of distance education, but sought to indicate who could offer it and the way mechanisms of control should be structured. Along these lines, we question what is understood as "self-learning". We believe that the student, upon choosing distance education, will have to assume great responsibility for what they learn, characterized by autonomy and discipline by some authors, especially when the time is flexible. Nevertheless, we find it relevant to emphasize that following the student, especially in formal educational processes, is fundamental for their development.

Still with respect to the decree, it was determined that all institutions credentialed to offer distance education could do so according to the criteria established two months later, in Article 2 of Decree 301, on April 7, 1998.

On October 18, 2001, Decree 2.253 was granted, which allowed the development of non-face-to-face courses in recognized face-to-face undergraduate programs, even if the institution is not credentialed to offer distance education. According to this decree, courses can be conducted in part or entirely using non-face-to-face resources, composing up to 20% of total course hours needed to fulfill requirements for completion of the program.

According to Fragale Filho (2003, p.20), this "decree ended up creating a numerical level which, once passed, transforms a face-to-face course into a non-face-to-face course, i.e. a distance course." Analyzing this possibility, he notes that

> [...] this means that we dealing with the partial offer of non-face-to-face contents under the name of experimentalism, not including, in a strict sense, the universe relative to distance education, which is unfortunate, since the PNE[2] itself recommends striving for a clearer articulation between face-to-face and non-face-to-face teaching. (FRAGALE FILHO, 2003, p.20)

On December 19, 2005, Decree 5.622 was passed which introduced, in Article 1, a new concept of distance education:

> Distance education is characterized as an educational modality in which the didactic-pedagogical mediation in the teaching-learning processes occurs with the use of information and communication means and technologies, with students and teachers developing educational activities in diverse times and places.

In addition, the following are still required: students' occasional on-site presence for examinations; obligatory internships and defenses of end-of-course projects, when described in the pertinent legislation; and activities related to teaching laboratories. Levels of teaching at which distance education can be offered are also defined, highlighting that "distance courses and programs should be projected to have the same duration defined for the respective face-to-face courses".

Other aspects were also addressed in this decree, showing a normative concern regarding questions related to distance education. Some points still remain to be addressed, but these will appear based experiences realized in this modality.

SOME CONCEPTIONS OF DISTANCE EDUCATION

Face-to-face teaching is rooted in our lives. Associated with it is the practice developed based solely on physical presence and meetings of the people involved in the process. Therefore, regular days, locales, and times are usually established (MORAN, 2002).

On the other hand, what are the principal characteristics of distance education? For Torres (2004, p.60), it is a

> [...] systematic form of education that uses technical means and bidirectional/multidirectional communication technologies with the purpose of promoting autonomous learning through a dialogical and collaborative relation between equidistant students and teachers.

For Gonzalez (2005), principal characteristics of distance education include the separation between teacher and student in space and/or time; greater student control over their own learning; and communication mediated by printed documents or some form of technology.

Moran (2002, p.1) describes it as follows: "distance education may or may not include face-to-face encounters, but it takes place fundamentally with teachers and students physically separated in space and/or time, but able to be together through communication technology". This is the conception that we have adopted. Thus, the focus is not on the number of face-to-face hours, but on the possibility for interaction at a distance among the actors in the process, mediated by technology. Bringing together people who are geographically distant, possibly creating a space for exchange between different cultures, is a central factor that defines this modality of teaching.

The Internet opened up a range of possibilities for courses offered via distance, changing ways of thinking about and doing distance education, and according to Valente (2003a, 2003b), current models are differentiated by the degree of interaction between teachers and students.

There are proposals denominated "one-to-one" in which the material is provided in a format similar to a book for the student to study individually with little or no contact with the teacher. Student evaluation is carried out afterwards based on a standardized test. In this case, the Internet is the source of information, and it is up to the student to transform it into knowledge. Courses of this type serve a large number of students and tend to generate large profits for their organizers. If we think of continuing teacher education, we can affirm that this type of course does not privilege the role of interaction in the professional development of teachers. It is similar to what Valente calls the broadcast approach.

Other proposals are defined by interactions that occur in a manner similar to traditional face-to-face classes, in which the teacher assigns activities that are developed and handed in by the students. Much of the interaction is limited to the exchange of questions and answers, in a relation known as "one-to-many". Some experiences in distance education have been developed in this way, as an adaptation of face-to-face classes, with "new clothes", but can be considered obsolete by current day standards. Valente calls this approach the virtualization of traditional school.

In the "many-to-many" approach, interaction is more intense, with the possibility for rapid feedback via the Internet, in synchronous and asynchronous activities that allow communication between the student and teacher as well as among students. In this scenario, the teacher follows the students closely, challenging them and encouraging their participation in the group, which Valente calls being together virtually[3].

Before these classifications became known, authors such as Borba and Penteado (2001) were already warning against "domesticating" a medium like the Internet, saying that the new possibilities provided by such technologies should be taken advantage of. Based on previous experiences with the use of software in face-to-face environments (BORBA, 1999a), Borba and Penteado proposed distance courses that included a strong emphasis on interaction, exploiting all the possibilities in this sense. They pointed to a model for distance courses, developed since 2000, based on chat rooms, e-mail, and traditional mail. This model has been expanded and transformed since that time, incorporating other interfaces like forums and videoconferences with the aid of instant communicators and mobile phones for emergencies, and always emphasizing communication among course participants.

Regardless of the model adopted, technological media are necessary to enable communication. These are commonly referred to as Virtual Learning Environments (VLE) and constitute a scenario in which teaching and learning can take place in qualitatively different ways depending on the resources at hand. When using a VLE with audio and video resources, for example, the possibilities are very different from one in which the interaction takes place through writing only, by means of chat.

Resources of asynchronous communication include discussion lists, portfolios, and forums, which enable students to express their questions and ideas and share their solutions to problems each in their own time. With synchronous interaction tools, like chat and videoconference, it is possible to share ideas in real time even when people are not in the same physical location.

We believe that synchronous and asynchronous interactions are important in online distance education as long as there is collaboration among the participants. The nature of the learning is qualitatively different when there is interaction, depending on its intensity and quality, and the curriculum should be organized taking into consideration the possibilities offered by the media used.

According to Belloni's (2003) characterization, the concept of interaction originates from sociology, and is a process in which at least two human actors are present who relate to each other simultaneously (i.e. synchronously) or at different times (asynchronously). It is an elementary phenomenon of human relations, which include educational relations. Thus, it differs from interactivity, as the latter is associated with the possibility of interacting with a machine.

Considering the concepts interaction and interactivity, we note that Information and Communication Technologies (ICTs) have broadened the possibilities in the sphere of online distance education. With increasingly advanced programs, modern interfaces, and possibilities for rapid feedback, as well as the range of hypertexts available on the Internet, interactivity has been intensified. However, this interactivity is often limited to the relation between the student and the informational content accessed via CD-ROMS or websites, for example.

Interaction via the Internet, in turn, makes it possible to combine various possibilities of human interaction, through the use of different software and interfaces, with freedom in relation to time and space. The relations between students and the various elements that make up the educational scenario, such as content, the teacher, other students, the teaching institution, etc., are situated in this context.

Thus, the physical absence of the teacher is compensated for by intense communication which limits the possibility that the student will feel alone or isolated. To avoid this, their questions are answered in a timely manner and their participation is constantly encouraged.

For Silva (2003a), the possibility of interaction is not simply yet another product of the digital age, but rather a new communication paradigm that is gradually substituting the transmission paradigm that characterizes mass media communication. Interaction demands that we re-think the traditional media and the role of the actors involved in the process.

COLLABORATION IN ONLINE EDUCATION

With the advance of the Internet, online distance education proposals have emphasized the dialogical process made possible by the **tools** available on the web that enable communication in real or deferred time. Silva (2003b) calls our attention to the fact that, in order for interaction in a distance course to be effective, at least three fundamental aspects must be satisfied. One is collaborative participation, understood as participation that is not limited to "yes" or "no", but which aims to intervene in the communication process, making one a co-creator of the emission and reception. Another refers to bi-directionality and the dialogic relationship itself, since the communication that develops in a course should be produced jointly by the students and the teacher who participate in the emission and reception, and who are poles who codify and de-codify. The third aspect is the existence of connections in open webs, which emphasizes that communication assumes multiple articulated networks that enable free exchange, association, and meaning-making.

We think these aspects are important, and similar to Valente's "being together virtually", our proposals for online distance education have been structured, since 2000, on the conception that interaction, dialogue, and collaboration are the factors that condition the nature of the learning. It is our belief that the quality of online distance education is directly related to these aspects, as they determine the quality of the participation of the people involved during the process of knowledge production.

When the focus is mathematical learning, interaction is a necessary condition in the process. Exchanging ideas, sharing possible solutions for a problem, and presenting one's rationale are actions that make up mathematical "doing". And to develop the process at a distance, models that enable the involvement of many people have gained ground in relation to those that focus in individuality.

In this sense, dialogue is seen as a process of discovery influenced by collective action and sharing. Thus, it is not constituted merely of the act of people communicating, but of the depth and richness of this act. Dialogue is a process that goes beyond simple conversation (ALRØ; SKOVSMOSE, 2006). To produce knowledge, it is important to perceive the importance of people expressing their opinions, sharing their experiences and feelings such as insecurity, fear, and doubt. In the same way, one must know how to value the participation of the other, listening respectfully to what is shared.

Freire (2005) points out that it is not through silence that people constitute themselves, but among other factors, through words. For him, dialogue is based on the encounter between humans for the common task of knowing how to act, mediated by the world, and it imposes itself as the path by which they acquire meaning as people. Thus, it cannot be reduced to "the act of depositing the ideas of one subject in another, nor become the simple act of exchanging ideas to be consumed by the exchangers" (p. 93).

Nor can it be a war between people who want to impose their truths rather than seek them together. "The conquest implicit in dialogue is of the world by the dialogical subjects, and not of one over the other. [...] Authentic education is not done by 'A' **for** 'B', or by 'A' **over** 'B', but by 'A' **with** 'B'" (p. 93, authors' emphasis). Thus, Freire emphasizes that the dialogical act cannot have arrogant positions, but requires humility. Also, "there is no true dialogue if there is, in its subjects, no true thinking. Critical thinking. [...] Without dialogue, there is no communication, and without this, there is no true education" (p.97-98)

Alrø and Skovsmose (2006) state that the quality of learning is intimately linked to the quality of communication. The relations between people are crucial to facilitating learning, as learning is a personal act but is shaped in a context of interpersonal relations, and dialogue, as a means if interaction, enables the mutual enrichment of people.

Ideas like these regarding the importance of dialogical relations have inhabited education and mathematics education for some time, as can be seen in the seminal works of authors such as Paulo Freire and Bicudo (1979), respectively. This makes them highly relevant for the online distance education scenario, since communication, synchronous as well as asynchronous, must be permeated with this deeper notion of dialogue, in which participants open up to one another using the interfaces available in a given virtual environment.

Considering collaboration as part of the interactive process, teacher and students should act as partners in the mathematical learning process. It differs from cooperation in that it goes beyond simply helping one's classmate to carry out a task. Authors such as Fiorentini (2004), Hargreaves (2001), Kenski (2003), Miskulin et al. (2005), Guérios (2005), and Nacarato (2005) point to issues involving different aspects of collaboration, and emphasize that, in a collaborative process, everyone actively participates. Activities are carried out collectively in such a way that the task of one complements the task of the other, since in collaboration, all are aiming to achieve common objectives by working together and mutually supporting one another.

When a group develops collaboratively, its members are not interested in doing tasks and engaging in activities for their own benefit, but rather establish common goals permeated by reciprocity. Ferreira and Miorim (2003, p.17) note that "collaboration means assuming joint responsibility for the process. It means taking turns, having a voice, and being listened to; it means feeling one is a member of something that only works because everyone works and builds the road collectively to achieve the objectives".

The option to belong to a group is influenced by the identification of a person with other members of the group, as well as the possibility of sharing problems, experiences, and common objectives. Trust is a basic ingredient to building a group in which the creation of collaborative work relations is meaningful, and this trust is based on dialogue, loyalty, and reciprocity in moments of decision making.

Collaboration is determined by the internal will of each individual to work together with the other and to be part of a given group. In this way, relations tend to be spontaneous, voluntary, guided by development, spread over time and space, and unpredictable.

However, exchanging experiences, sharing solutions to problems proposed, and joint action do not imply thinking in a uniform fashion. It is an environment of contribution in which individuals join forces in the search for collective benefit. The collective is not necessarily synonymous with solid and uniform, since as a group, the individuality of its members is respected in such a way that, based on their differences, they produce and grow together.

In heterogeneity, different forms of relations among equals are established which, in the process of working as a group, are needed to manage conflicts, propose alternatives, review concepts, take positions, divide up the work, re-think ideas, etc. Thus, a collaborative group can promote exchange and learning without losing the individuality of each member and without having to arrive at a single, uniform perspective.

This process does not prevent each member from having their own point of view and distinct interests, but rather benefits from different contributions based on different levels of participation. Collaboration also does not imply that everyone participates in the same way. Each makes their own voice heard from where they are at, but everyone works together. We know that teacher and student have distinct roles in the learning process, and what we want to emphasize is that each can participate actively in their own way throughout the process.

From the perspective of teacher education, experiences with distance courses like those analyzed by Gracias (2003), Bairral (2005), and Zulatto and Borba (2006) have shown that commitment and collaboration tend to flow when individual interests are respected and valued, since these factors significantly influence the quality of discussion in a VLE.

Mutual support among group members is a fundamental factor to survival in a collaborative environment. Respect for different conceptual knowledge and the experiences of every future teacher, as well as their difficulties, is indispensable to the learning process. They need to feel that their practice is valued and that they have the support of the others as well as the teacher as they try, collaboratively, to find a solution to a problem or question.

In this context, members of a collaborative group assume the role of protagonists as they become actors in the production of knowledge, learning as well as teaching, without being limited to being mere providers of information and materials. They are different voices, positions, and shared experiences that can contribute to the improvement of teaching practice. Collaboration among teachers demands a group synergy that allows knowledge production to take place simultaneously with the personal and professional development of the group members.

We consider education, particularly of future teachers, to be a movement of process, which is justified by our understanding that movements of formal education occur at precise moments, whereas the reaction does not, since formal moments fertilize the teacher's practice, impelling them to new ways of doing things. Thus, it is as though each immediate action corresponds to a reaction that is not only immediate. The effects of formal education are reflected in the teacher's entire professional process, intermingled with other reactions provoked by other experiences, formal or otherwise, that acquire significance when they are reflected in teaching practice.

Knowledge produced in formal educational moments interacts with the teacher's life, in the professional and personal dimensions, and should produce an internal movement that provokes a process of transformations in the teacher. We understand that continuing education is a course that can be interpreted "as an unique and continuous path, which leads us to the conjecture that in this path, transformations occur, provoked by the interaction between formal stages of education and experientiality, in the dynamic of the collective everyday" (GUÉRIOS, 2005, p.136).

Thus, continuing teacher education should consider relevant aspects of teachers' professional experience and provide them with the opportunity to reflect constantly and critically on their practice. The teaching process can constitute spaces for this reflection, as well as compel the teacher to develop their capacity for intuition, raising hypotheses, reflection, analysis, organization, etc.

From this perspective, collaborative work can become an important scenario for teachers' professional development, in a way that the group assumes a fundamental role in processes of producing knowledge and reflection. This appropriation or internalization, however, is an individual process which does not depend only on shared moments, but on the professional development of each person, as well.

In this sense, like Perez et al. (2002), we believe in continuing education in which reflection on teaching practice, collaboration, and discussion are crucial elements, and teachers are provided with the conditions to face, individually and collectively, new and different learning situations. As we intend to show, it is our belief that online distance education brings new possibilities to continuing education, whether in the form of courses or of virtual communities oriented toward exchange. Consequently, the practicing teacher can interact with colleagues and specialists throughout Brazil and the world without leaving their work environment.

Therefore, teachers' professional development and reflexive practice become the principal elements guiding continuing education in a way that considers them to be subjects in their own education and leads them to realize the importance of their teaching practice in the professional development process.

Continuing education can also constitute a process that broadens conditions for exchanging experiences and seeking innovations and solutions to problems that emerge in the everyday life of the school. Using teachers' experience as the starting point for continuing education does not imply denial of the knowledge produced by educational sciences, but rather to consider practice as the starting point and finish line of the educational process. In this way, formal educational experiences become a space for reflection.

In the continuing education experiences that we organized in GPIMEM, face-to-face as well as distance, we were attentive to these considerations and sought to provide an environment of exchange that led to a collaborative educational process and learning. We worked within this perspective influenced by our conception of the role of the teacher in education processes, especially in online distance education.

Silva calls our attention to the fact that teachers need to prepare themselves for the role of teacher in an online distance education environment:

> Rather than merely teaching, the teacher will have to learn to make multiple experimentations and expressions available, as well as creating networks that allow multiple occurrences. Rather than merely transmitting, he will be a formulator of problems, provoker of situations, architect of routes, mobilizer of the experience of knowledge. (SILVA, 2003b, p.12)

In this quote, one observes that many of the characteristics described are also desirable for teachers in a face-to-face class. For authors like Maia

(2002), there is no difference between the teacher who works in a face-to-face situation and one who teaches distance courses. Both should have the basic characteristics needed to carry out the role of teacher, beginning with the premise that they are willing to share specific knowledge with a group of students, and therefore, their attention should be centered on learning, with a pedagogical proposal the includes relevant aspects such as the means of communication, the methodology, and others.

One could say, therefore, that the professional is the same; that a teacher who teaches face-to-face courses can also teach distance courses, and vice versa. However, the teacher needs to pay attention to her teaching practice which, focused on learning, must be adapted to a new environment and new pedagogical proposal that requires a different methodology from that used in a face-to-face class. For some authors, these changes demand a characteristic approach that gives life to a "new professional" who, according to Kenski (2003, p.143), "must act and be different in the virtual environment. This necessity is due to the very specificity of cyberspace, which makes possible new forms, new spaces, and new times for teaching, interaction, and communication among everyone". He emphasizes that the teacher's competence should shift toward encouraging learning and thinking, becoming the animator who incites students to exchange ways of knowing and to guide, in a personalized way, the course of the learning. It is important to propose tasks, establish reading lists, etc., so that the student feels the teacher's presence even in a virtual learning environment.

Thus, it continues to be the teacher who defines the contents of the course and conducts it or, in some cases, the company administering the course (face-to-face or online) may define the contents, taking this right away from the teacher. In a differentiated pedagogical perspective, in which students have the possibility to explore the content collaboratively, or to pursue their own interests, the curricular structure and the teacher cannot be rigid. Thus, the communication cannot be one-way, from teacher to student, but in various directions, from student to student, student to students, teacher to student, and teacher to students.

Prado and Almeida (2003) point out that the role of the teacher is not specifically that of the source of information, but mainly of adviser and partner in learning, considering the ideas and particularities of the students. The teacher therefore needs to assume different roles, as mediator, observer, articulator: "His main function is to **guide students' learning** – learning that develops through **collaborative interaction** [...], facilitating the creation of a network of communication and collaboration in which everyone interrelates" (p. 72, author's emphasis).

Some authors still emphasize that the administration of an online course, at first glance, seems easy, however most demand more preparation time and involvement than conventional courses. As an example, one can think of the need to visit the virtual environment or website of the course daily, more than once a day if possible, so that students feel supported by the teacher. This demands a considerable amount of time. Based on the examples given, we will be specifying other competencies that online teachers should have, which are conditioned by the interface being used, and differ depending on the main means of communication – chat or videoconference, for example.

Therefore, it is essential to highlight that the use of computer technology demands, at least at first, a considerable time commitment from the teacher to prepare activities, plan, and attend to students, which must be constant so as to avoid discouraging students. And participation in courses for professional development and to remain up to date also demands time. The teacher must be familiar with the technological tool being used, which does not necessarily dispense with the need for a technician who can provide support to resolve problems with equipment, if necessary.

In this context, like Zulatto (2007), we understand that student and teacher, together with the technologies they use, walk hand-in-hand in the production of knowledge, considering that

> **collaborative online learning** is a process in which students, teachers, and technology participate actively and interact at a distance to produce meanings collectively, raising uncertainties that encourage the search for understandings and raising new uncertainties. In this way, humans and media plan and develop actions that are of interest to a group, respecting the individualities, to produce knowledge collaboratively in cyberspace (p. 70, author's emphasis)

Using a camera as a metaphor, we can consider the above quote to be a provisory synthesis when we zoom in with the camera, and when we zoom out, it transforms into an entire community that is interested in transforming itself as new technological possibilities are offered.

We believe new technologies are not to be feared or idolatrized. ICTs transform our lives and change collaborative thinking and practice in continuing education courses and in other practices involving educators in the virtual world. On the other hand, we can shape the way online education becomes consolidated in Brazil and in the world, in the particular context of mathematics education. In this sense, we are fighting so that models based on interaction among participants prevail over mass models that are mainly profit-oriented and based on a vision of education as a commodity.

DISTANCE MATHEMATICS EDUCATION USING CHAT

In the preceding chapter, we presented some elements related to online distance education, such as interaction, collaboration, dialogue, continuing education, and the role of the teacher, and we discussed how they are important for knowledge production in distance courses. In the context of mathematics, in particular, we showed how different media can transform the nature of this field of knowledge, based on examples from research.

In mathematics education, various studies have explored the possibilities of using chat as an interface, including Bairral (2002; 2004; 2005), Bello (2004), Lopes (2004), and others. In all of them, courses conducted via chat rooms and other interfaces were proffered to high school and university students as well as practicing teachers with the objective of investigating issues related to student assessment in online distance education, construction of mathematical knowledge on a given content, and others. For this, course models were elaborated based on perspectives related to the objectives of the studies as well as the view of knowledge of the course organizers.

GPIMEM, as described by Borba and Penteado (2001), began researching models for online distance education courses some time ago that converged with the group's conception regarding teaching and learning based on aspects such as dialogue and the premise that knowledge is produced by collectives of human and non-human actors. In addition to pedagogical issues, the available technology was also taken into consideration due to the dependence on existing resources on the UNESP[1]-Rio Claro campus to carry out the educational model adopted. The first university extension course was offered in 2000, entitled Trends in Mathematics Education, proffered entirely via distance by professors and researchers in the group. Since then, new versions of the course have been developed and offered annually for teachers of mathematics and related fields. Changes have been made over the years related to technical as well as pedagogical issues[2].

Based on our experiences and research, we will present a portrait in this chapter of some of our experiences in these courses, discussing the educational model we adopted and highlighting aspects related to chat and the mathematical discussions that took place using chat.

IN SEARCH OF A MODEL

Among various courses offered by GPIMEM, the Trends in Mathematics Education course can be considered to be a different kind of practice, as new versions of the courses were created and transformed in accordance with the new interests and experiences of the professors and researchers involved.

In the initial version offered in 2000, a chat resource was used that was available for free on a web page, in which the moderator could control access to the discussions through a registration system. A homepage was created as a complement to function as a bulletin board for posting information such as course syllabus and bibliographic references for the teacher-students[3]. In addition, a discussion list, via e-mail, was also used for asynchronous communication among participants. We did not have access to virtual learning environments at that time, which later became available for free.

Versions of the Trends[4] course, structured in this way, were successfully carried out and were the subject of study for researchers such as Gracias (2003), who addressed the nature of the reorganization of thinking based on the technologies employed as well as the pedagogical model adopted. Nevertheless, we sought different alternatives, including options for simultaneous interaction and information. Based on studies and pilot tests, we opted initially for TelEduc[5], a VLE that offers a range of options, with tools like forum, portfolio, discussion lists, bulletin board, chat, and others. With TelEduc, the nature of the course was changed based on the technological possibilities it provided. Research was carried out based on the versions of the Trends course that were offered in this VLE, including Borba (2004) and Santos (2006).

Nevertheless, in 2006, we migrated to another environment, TIDIA-Ae[6]. The decision to change emerged as a result of our group's collaboration in the development of this platform, which we saw as an opportunity to participate in the design of the environment. Taking advantage of our specialized knowledge, we have contributed suggestions to the developers with the aim of building a free environment that can be used for different activities in various fields of knowledge. In addition, the version-in-progress of TIDIA-Ae has some innovative tools, such as hypertext, which is a collaborative, asynchronous text editor.

In our view, there is no ideal model of environment for conducting courses of this nature, since the resources offered by each platform are distinct, making different options available to users. We believe that there is a virtual environment that adapts most coherently to the context according to the objectives established in advance. It is up to the organizer of the activities to analyze the pros and cons of each of the interfaces available. Issues related to the technology used should also be considered as one thinks about a course or the actions to be carried out using these platforms.

Based on our experiences as educators and organizers of distance courses, we were faced with the possibilities and the limitations of the platforms used (BORBA et al., 2005). In the context of mathematics education, these difficulties are strongly related to the very nature of the mathematical language, with is characterized by particularities that often make discussion difficult. For example, if we have a given problem whose sentence would be given by $\int_{2}^{4}\left(\frac{1}{x^2} + x\right)dx$, we would have to write "the integral defined in the interval of two to four of the function one over x squared plus x", or "integral of 2 to 4 of 1 over x squared + x dx". As we write the sentence, regardless of the manner chosen, in addition taking longer for the participant to interpret it and translate it into mathematical symbols, it can lead to mistakes, as it is well known that people often write informally in chat and use abbreviations to save time.

Initially, the objective of the Trends course was to present and discuss some of the existing areas of research in mathematics education, such as teacher education, ICTs, and mathematical modeling. The intention was to provide the teacher-students with an initial understanding of what research in mathematics education is and its different areas of study. In the process, we also began to ask what would happen when mathematical topics were discussed via chat. What would a mathematical discussion be like in a chat? Would mathematics be transformed in a virtual environment? Thus, beginning in 2002 when the course was being offered for the third time, we began to discuss mathematics in chat rooms based on activities developed within an experimental-with-technologies perspective, in which students (teacher-students, in our case) act together with software to generate, conjecture, and present solutions to a given problem.

The dynamic of these courses consists mainly of the teacher-students reading texts assigned by the professor prior to each synchronous meeting selected from a list of required as well as optional readings on the themes to be discussed in class. These synchronous meetings, which last an average of approximately three hours, are conducted via chat. Two debaters are chosen prior to each class to stimulate discussion and are responsible for presenting questions to their colleagues. The presence of the debaters does not prevent the other participants of the professors from raising issues during the class; rather, their role is to stimulate discussion, providing them with the opportunity to practice "leadership" in activities of this nature. In this way, we believe we are contributing to the educational experience of teachers who may be proffering distance courses themselves in the future, an issue pointed out by Borba (2004) as being important. At the end of each session, one of the teacher-students is given responsibility for writing a summary of the class and making it available to the others. Due to the course structure described here, the number of participants is limited to 25 so that everyone can "speak" and "be listened to". On occasion, when possible, we invite the authors of the texts being debated to participate in the discussions. Another practice we have adopted is to occasionally ask specialists on the themes being discussed to take part in the class as invited guests, enriching the debate.

For those classes in which the theme to be discussed was a specific mathematical content, activities were planned and made available ahead of time to the teacher-students. Activities involving the use of software generally made use of open-source software; in the case of Geometricks[7], which was used in one of the versions of the course, participants had the option of purchasing the software or using a free demo version.

As the reader can see, the model adopted for the course is in synergy with our proposals as well as intimately related with our view of knowledge, as we believe that the act of learning is not passive, and that interaction between professors and students in debates is fundamental. It is thus up to the professors to identify those who are not engaging in discussions and question them. This has been a constant practice in the courses offered by GPIMEM since 2000.

Over the course of the meetings, the teacher-students come to realize that the prior readings are fundamental to be able to participate in the discussions, and that due to the dynamic of the course as well as the nature of chat, there are no long explanations or talks on given themes. The reader may be asking at this point, "Why due to the nature of chat?" Discussions in chat rooms have qualitatively different characteristics than those that take place in other learning environments, virtual or otherwise. As mentioned in the introduction, there is a tendency in chat for multilogue to occur, i.e. simultaneous conversations on subjects directly or indirectly related to the main focus of the meeting, with participants sometimes involved in more than one discussion, or "jumping" from one to another. We know that the word "dialogue" characterizes a conversation between two or more people; thus, the idea of multilogue is related to the multiplicity of dialogues taking place at the same time in a chat session. In addition, they are not linear, in the sense that questions and responses do not appear sequentially on the screen. Borba and Penteado (2001), for example, to illustrate a multilogue, presented an excerpt from a chat session using different fonts to highlight the different dialogues going on in order to help the reader.

With this multiplicity of simultaneous conversations, it is often difficult for the professor, as well as the teacher-students, to follow them all and give feedback. This dynamic changes the very nature of the production of knowledge, which is conditioned by the interaction that takes place in a chat room. Those who have never taken part in this type of discussion feel lost and confused at first; however, participants appeared to adapt "naturally", since after a few meetings, they no longer mentioned having problems with the "avalanche" of information and questions occurring simultaneously.

Up to this point we have been discussing, in some detail, issues related to the model we adopted for the course and some of the consequences. We would still like to highlight how discussion occurs via chat during activities related to a specific field of knowledge, mathematics. In the section that follows, we will provide examples that illustrate some specific aspects of the discussion and production of mathematics using chat.

First, however, we would like to emphasize that professors who teach using chat rooms must cope with new demands. They must be prepared to deal with various questions at the same time, referring to distinct aspects of the theme under debate. In our courses, professors commonly need to handle different questions at the same time during a mathematics education class, since the teacher-students ask questions without having read the questions of the others. For example, texts A and B are being debated during a given meeting. Even when the professor decides, after dialoguing with students, to initiate the discussion with text B, it is not uncommon for questions to be raised about text A. Gracias (2003) illustrates this well. In mathematics classes, there is a need to follow different lines of reasoning on a given problem simultaneously; and when the professor, for some reason, allows a question to go by unnoticed, participants protest emphatically. Knowing how to handle these demands, as well as having the ability to type quickly and read the messages on the screen at the same time, appear to be important skills for this type of teaching. As we will see, special demands also emerge when dealing with mathematics, especially geometry, when participants do not share a common screen, as in one of the examples that follows.

MATHEMATICAL PROBLEMS IN CHAT

Examples of Functions

When we consider virtual discussions about mathematics, questions arise regarding the type of activities we should propose to the teacher-students. Borba (2004; 2005) offered some reflections in this regard, providing evidence that there are pedagogical approaches that may be more appropriate and adapted to the possibilities provided by the Internet. Since, as outlined in Chapter I, our view is that knowledge is the product of a collective and dialogue, interaction and collaboration, and that these are factors that condition learning, we believe that open, exploratory activities are in synergy with virtual educational practice.

Based on these premises, activities were elaborated in which teacher-students were encouraged to use mathematical software, like Winplot[8], for example, to explore conjectures based on plotted functions.

Activities with specific mathematical contents were introduced in the third version of the Trends course, with discussions involving functions and

Euclidean geometry. Other mathematical topics, like fractals, spatial Euclidean geometry, and mathematical models, were explored in later versions of the course. In the case of fractals, the debates followed a model similar to the readings-based mathematics education classes, as it was a new theme for most participants, and the class was based on another book from this series written by Barbosa (2002).

In one class in which the theme was functions, one of the proposed activities was based on the graph below (FIG. 1). Participants received only a Word file containing the graph and were asked to find the algebraic expression that represents it using graphing software to "experiment" and deduce.

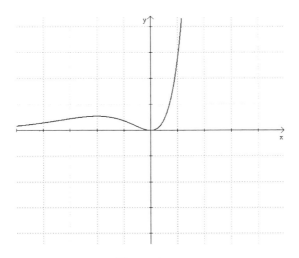

Figure 1

The professor, who is the first author of this book, presented one of the objectives of the activity: "The [...] proposal of the activity is to be able to present a problem originating from the graph and not the algebra", i.e., the activity consisted of finding the algebraic expression for the graph. At the very beginning of the discussion, one of the teacher-students asked, "... how do I enter functions defined by multiple expressions in Winplot?" The professor then provided a clue, saying that the law of function is not composed of various expressions, but rather a product of functions. The discussion that ensued is presented below. Note that the professor is identified as mborba in some excerpts and as MarceloBorba in others, and the others are teacher-students.

The time the comments were written appear in parentheses[9].

(20:30:53) Nilceia: It's the product of a quadratic and a trigonometric?

(20:31:35) Luiza: This one is really difficult. You can see is that we have one curve for x < 0 and another for x > 0, and that in one of the cases, it can also be equal to zero.

(20:32:57) mborba: That's half correct, Nilceia! But what led you to think that?

(20:34:08) Nilceia: The design of the graph.

(20:34:28) Eliane: If it were the sum of functions, I would have thought it was a straight line and a parabola, but product really does seem to have to do with trigonometric.

(20:36:00) mborba: Why trigonometric and not second degree, Eliane?

(20:36:28) Eliane: In a sum, if the line were increasing and passed through zero, the result before the origin would be "pulled down", like it is in the graph.

(20:37:13) Eliane: Both trigonometric and parabola, as well.

(20:37:56) mborba: Eliane, but so what explains the little "upturn" it makes close to negative 2 and zero? (20:38:36) mborba: Give it a try, Nilceia!

(20:38:43) Eliane: You'd have to test it to see; just looking at it can fool you a lot!

(20:38:55) mborba: Actually, Eliane, between negative 4 and zero.

(20:41:23) Nilceia: So tell me, then: which part is correct?

(20:43:16) mborba: If I had a better clue to give you, I would, of course, but I don't. I never proposed this activity to anyone before, although I explained the objectives before […].

(20:44:12) Eliane: $y = x\sin(x)*x^\wedge 2$ I did this and it gave a parabola in the middle and two almost vertical straight lines on the sides.

In the above excerpt, we can notice that the teacher-students were using visual aspects of the graph to conjecture about the possible law of the function. However, one of the participants, after the professor's "clue", felt the need to do a test, experimenting with software, saying that observation alone was insufficient. For this reason, she opened Winplot and drew a graph of the function $f(x) = x.\text{sen}(x).x^2$, illustrating that experimentation also takes place simultaneously with the chat discussion. We can also note that the way teacher-students wrote the laws of the functions mathematically using chat is the same used to insert a function in Winplot, making it one of the mathematical languages used in chat. In this sense, it appears to be natural for teacher-students to use the software's language in the chat session.

Since there was a pause in the discussion at this point, the professor suggested presenting the answer to the problem. The reactions to this varied:

(20:50:32) Eliane: Is there any way you could give the answer and wait just a minute to test it in Winplot?

(20:50:44) Nilceia: Yes, but please explain how we arrived at this conclusion.

(20:50:53) mborba: Of course, Eliane. . and I will give it to you little by little.

(20:51:56) Carlos: Borba, I tried many things, but I couldn't find the answer, and I'm dying of curiosity. What should the teacher do when students get tired of trying and give up?

(20:52:28) mborba: Carlos, I think you should tell them, especially because this is very exploratory.

Based on what the teacher-students say, one can note different positions. Eliane, for example, wanted the answer so she could use it to get a glimpse of a possible solution based on experimentation with software. Nilcéia was also less worried about the answer itself than understanding the solution found by the professor. It is worth noting that, as the above excerpt shows, the teacher-students were willing to think about the activity, and the mere presentation of the solution did not satisfy them, whereas exploring did. After a few comments had been posted, the professor presented the solution to the problem:

(20:52:07) mborba: The "little belly" is because the parabola, which I already said is part of the product, interacts with the other function in the interval [-4,0] in a way that the former "still has power"; later it no longer does.

(20:53:38) mborba: In other words, the function "defeats" the second degree function in the rest of the negative interval, and "coincides", it has "synergy" with the parabola and the exponential e^x, or with another base greater than one . . . so then the size of the "little belly" will vary.

(20:54:42) mborba: [...] but here I thought I could say something right away so you guys could evaluate this type of activity and test the function $y=e^x(x^2)$.

(20:54:58) Eliane: Now I understand, cuz it begins to increase after the axis and keeps going and accelerates the growth of the parabola even more. Cool . . .

(20:55:08) mborba: Note that this informal way of talking about the graph should only be at first.

(20:55:47) mborba: What "it" are you referring to, Eliane? The product, for sure, because the exponential is always increasing, with a base greater than one.

(20:56:54) Nilceia: To arrive at this conclusion, do I need to test various graphs?

(20:57:48) Eliane: Sorry, it becomes greater than one, so the product becomes increasingly greater than the value of the parabola itself, which does not happen before the y-axis, because the exponential is less than one, and the product, although increasing, makes the parabola go down.

(20:57:54) mborba: Nilceia, I think that it could be one way for us to learn about functions, about their behavior. In fact, the second graph is a continuation of the first . . . except with something we are much less accustomed to.

At this point, the professor asked the teacher-students how the questions presented up until that moment could be formalized, which led to other discussions about aspects related to the software and its use in the classroom, how to make the "bridge" between exploration and formalization, etc.

We interpret the law of this function as being the product of the two functions when x tends toward $+\infty$ or $-\infty$. In the first case, the two functions are increasing and positive, and $\lim\limits_{x \to +\infty} e^x = \lim\limits_{x \to +\infty} x^2 = +\infty$. The product of these limits is always increasing, therefore $\lim\limits_{x \to +\infty} x^2.e^x = +\infty$. In the second case, a classic argument to explain the behavior of the product when $x \to -\infty$ is that the exponential function tends to zero "faster" than the quadratic function goes to $+\infty$, and since the exponential function is "stronger" than the polynomial function, the product of the two functions tends to zero.

Going back to the excerpt presented above, we can note that the approach of the course, which was developed using chat, focused not only on mathematical discussions, but also on educational issues related to this field of knowledge, characterizing a reflection on pedagogical practices based on the experiences of the teacher-students.

In another Trends course, the theme discussed was also functions, based on experimental activities. The problem being discussed had originated from a face-to-face class in an applied mathematics course for biology undergraduates at UNESP, Rio Claro. Using graphing calculators, students had been asked to vary the parameters a, b, and c of the function $f(x) = ax^2 + bx + c$, $a \neq 0$ and discuss the behavior of the graph. As they carried out the activity, a student named Renata had presented the following conjecture: whenever b is positive, the parabola will cross the y-axis with the increasing part of the parabola. Whenever it is negative, it will cross it with the decreasing portion of the parabola. Thus, we proposed to the teacher-students in the distance course that they investigate the parameters a, b, and c of the second degree function to explore Renata's statement and justify their responses.

One of the teacher-students, Carlos, began the debate by telling that he had proposed to his students that they also investigate the parameters a, b, and c with the help of Winplot, and that during the class, one of them had presented the following conjecture: "when a is negative, or b is positive, the parabola moves more to the right, but when a is negative and b is also negative, the parabola moves to the left". Since the student's hypothesis was intimately related to the activities we had proposed, we asked the teacher-students to discuss Carlos' student's conjecture, as well, and to emphasis the algebraic questions.

(19:53:15) MarceloBorba: The solution that Carlos' student gave regarding a and b; does anyone have an algebraic explanation for it?

(19:54:53) Taís: It has to do with the coordinate x of the vertex of the parabola.

(19:55:30) Carlos: After trying various times (they made various graphs varying the value of the a, b, and c coefficients), they concluded that the proposal in question 2 [presented by Renata, the biology student] was really valid.

The arguments presented differed. While Carlos affirmed that his students had concluded, through experimentation, that Renata's statement was correct, Taís presented evidence of a conclusion based on the formula of the vertex of the second degree function, i.e., she began to give an algebraic explanation for the problem. As we can observe in the discussion that followed, the arguments overlap:

(19:57:07) Taís: $Xv=-b/2a$...If a and b have different signs, Xv is positive.

(19:59:16) Norma: I made many graphs and verified it was true; afterwards, I went to the coordinates of the vertex of the parabola $Xv= -b / 2a$, and I analyzed the sign of b as a function of positive or negative a; then I checked the sign of the vertex crossing the concavity opening up or down and checking to see if it was on the increasing or decreasing part. I don't know if I made myself clear.

Norma and Taís presented similar ideas to confirm the biology student's conjecture. Sandra and Marcelo elaborated yet another justification for the statement based on the derivative of the second degree function, i.e. $f'(x) = 2.a.x + b$.

(20:00:43) Sandra: I understand, but I also understand that the increasing part of the parabola is when the first derivative is positive, i.e. for $x>-b/2a$.

(20:01:18) MarceloBorba: Why, Sandra? Say more about how you saw that!

(20:03:55) Sandra: If we have the equation $ax^2+bx+c= y$, then we have that $dy/dx = 2ax+b$, so if we want to know when the parabola is increasing, we have to calculate when $dy/dx >0$.

(20:05:04) Sandra: So, $x > - b/ 2a$.

(20:07:03) MarceloBorba: Sandra, except I saw it a bit differently. I saw calculating $y'(0)=b$, so when b is positive, the parabola will increase, and analogously . . .

Since few of the participants understood the explanation, Marcelo and Badin[10] explained the solution in greater detail.

(20:10:59) MarceloBorba: Sandra, upon calculating the value of y', I have that if y'>0, then the function is increasing, and therefore I take y'(0), which is equivalent to the point where y crosses the y-axis and [the function y'(0) =b, and so b decides it!!! Understand?

(20:13:43) Badin: The point where the graph "crosses" the y axis is f(0), therefore, to be in the increasing part of the parabola, we should consider two cases:

1. a>0: we should have the x of the vertex "before" the abscissa of the point where the graph crosses the y-axis, i.e. (-b/2a) <0. Since a>0, this occurs for b>0.

2. a<0: we should have the x of the vertex "after" the abscissa of the point where the graph crosses the y-axis, i.e. (-b/2a) >0. Since a<0, this occurs for b>0.

By this time, the teacher-students had been debating the problem and its solutions – vertex and derivative – for approximately 40 minutes. The time interval gaps in the transcriptions indicate where some parts were omitted to make it easier to follow the discussion. Other actors were involved in the debate and in refining the solutions to this problem, but we have opted to present only some of them for the sake of clarity.

We can highlight that the justifications for the conjectures presented via chat were written "naturally", using "natural language", given that the written word is the means of communication in a chat session. In addition, participants tried to make themselves understood through their "written words". In the face-to-face class, when Renata presented her conjecture, orality was the main actor in communication, and the students did not write their conclusions and justifications, but only spoke them. The professor of the Applied Mathematics class relied on the chalkboard to formalize Renata's conjecture, presenting the vertex solution to the class.

Example from Spatial Geometry

Some aspects of writing in chat are qualitatively different from writing with paper and pencil, and as we discuss mathematical questions in this environment, "doing" mathematics becomes transformed online. Writing, like multilogue, shapes the production of mathematical knowledge in different ways in online environments.

While this seemed reasonable when the content being addressed was functions, we decided to investigate what would happen with the mathematical discussion in the virtual world when the content was spatial geometry. Our research group was curious to know how the tension would play out between the model of the notion of space that most of us have, spatial geometry, and the Internet, which appears to destroy the notion of space and/or time that we had up until the end of the 20th Century, and constitutes a new notion. Readers interested in this theme can learn more by reading a detailed discussion in Santos (2006).

In 2005, the Trends course was the stage for this investigation about mathematical production in the chat room. Various trends in mathematics education were discussed in this edition of the course, led by the first author of this book, and Silvana Santos led discussions on mathematical activities. Her work (SANTOS, 2006) revealed various particularities of the nature of "doing" mathematics in the context of online distance education using diverse resources, such as manipulative materials, the free software *Wingeom*[11], as well as books on the subject. One of her conclusions emphasizes that, despite some limitations, the chat tool enabled discussion and made it possible for "mathematical production to become consolidated in a very specific way" (p.12). For her, these media conditioned the way the participants discussed the conjectures formulated during the geometrical constructions, thus transforming mathematical production. In her analysis, she highlighted the ways chat, the software, the coordinated use of different ICTs, investigation, and visualization are present and act in the production of mathematics in a distance course. Another aspect she emphasized is related to mathematical demonstration in a virtual environment, and to illustrate this ,we present an example. It should be noted that the activities proposed by Santos were of an investigative nature, and that the teacher-students were expected to use the Wingeom software to develop them.

In one of the problems, participants were asked to construct a rectangular parallelepiped and then sketch some segments and observe what would happen to the planes formed by points belonging to these segments and others belonging to their vertices. The statement of the problem[12] was as follows:

---

1. Insert a parallelepiped of length #, width 2 and height 6;

2. Using the menu Anim/Variation of # type, in the window that opens, 0 and then click fix L. In the same way, type 3 and click fix R;

3. Sketch segments AC, CH, and AH;

4. Click on See/Thickness of segment, select a color for the segments you sketched, and then click on add;

5. Sketch segments BE, EG, and BG;

6. As before, add a color for these segments;

7. Animate your construction and observe what happens;

8. What can you say about the planes defined by points ACH and BEG? Justify your answer.

9. What happens when the value of # is zero?

The Wingeom software has animation functions based on specific commands. The proposed activity requested fixed width and height for the parallelepiped, but the length could vary from 0 to 3. Thus, the solid could be "animated" based on the variation of its length. FIG. 2 illustrates the construction of this activity in Wingeom.

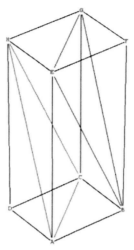

Figure 2

The chat discussion began when one of the participants, Maria, from Argentina, presented her conclusion: "In this activity, the conclusion I got was that the planes (GEB and HAC) are parallel (if #=0 are coincident), but I saw Marie's demonstration" (20:17:15). Marie, another teacher-student, had posted her demonstration earlier in the portfolio of TelEduc and referred to it again in the chat:

> (20:21:08) Marie: Look how I justified it: Planes ACH and BGE are parallel. We can justify it remembering that a straight line is parallel to a plane when it is parallel to a line on that plane. Considering that segment BG is parallel to segment AH (both diagonals of opposite and parallel faces of the parallelepiped) which belongs to plane ACH, we can state that segment BG is parallel to plane ACH. If we apply the same reasoning to segments EG and EB, we conclude that the planes are parallel.

> (20:22:22) Marie: Look at my figure in the portfolio. You can understand it better when you can visualize the figure.

> (20:22:28) Silvana: Marie, I don't understand . . . We can justify it remembering that a straight line is parallel to a plane when it is parallel to a line on that plane??? Sorry . . .

> (20:23:12) Marie: Yes, that's what descriptive geometry says.

(20:23:42) Maria: What Marie said is true: if a straight line is parallel to another on a plane, it is parallel to the plane (I have the Theorem here).

(20:23:52) Silvana: Ah, OK!!!

In this excerpt, we notice that Marie does note state that she demonstrated, but rather that she justified her conclusion, and she suggests that it is easier to understand if one looks at the figure she constructed and posted in the portfolio. Another point we would like to emphasize is related to the various resources used by the teacher-students. Silvana Santos, who was co-teaching the course, did not understand Marie's justification, and Maria, who had a book by her side when she said "I don't know all the theorems . . . I have the reference book next to me here!!! Ha!!!" (20:34:07), confirmed what Marie had said based on a theorem.

More arguments, doubts, and demonstrations were presented by the teacher-students as the debate continued:

(20:23:52) Dias: Marie, another doubt is noticeable that the planes GEF and...

(20:24:38) Claudia: Sil, we used the following, but I'm not sure
Def.: Two planes are parallel, if and only if they have no points in common or are equal.
Sufficient condition: EG and BG to the plane BEG and are concurrent, having AC and AH on plane ACH and EG // AC and BG // AH, plane EGB is parallel to ACH.

(20:24:48) Dias: ACH are "sub-planes" of parallel planes, but can we conclude from that that they are parallel?

(20:25:56) Maria: What is ACH "sub-planes"?

(20:26:15) Carlos: (a small correction) EG and BG belong to plane BEG and are concurrent, having AC and AH belonging to plane ACH and EG // AC and BG // AH, so planes EGB is parallel to ACH.

(20:26:21) Marie: Let's think in practical terms. You are probably in a room, right? Think of the walls as planes. Think of a door, and consider one of the door posts as a straight line. Isn't this "straight line" parallel to a straight line on the wall opposite the wall where the door is? Think of a straight line as where the walls meet. So then you can say that the door is parallel to the wall because it is parallel to the intersection of the two walls, which is considered a straight line. Is that clear, or did it confuse things more?

(20:28:31) Marie: Dias, planes are infinite...

In this excerpt, we can see that demonstration, in a chat, as Santos emphasized, is done "in pieces", in other words,

One part is presented and then another message appears from someone else, about the same subject or not, and meanwhile, the one who was presenting the demonstration is typing and presents another part, and the process repeats itself until the demonstration is concluded. (SANTOS, 2006, p.98)

In addition, Marie used a visual image to illustrate her conjectures and tried to get the other participants to "see" the figure. In response, others presented more statements, continuing the justifications posted earlier.

(20:29:50) Dias: from the same idea as subset. Taking the same example as Marie's: Take the wall that represents a plane and a chalkboard attached to it; the chalkboard is a plane subset of the wall.

(20:30:42) Silvana: Marie, I like your strategy of making things more "visible"...But let me think better about this door... haha.

(20:31:39) mborba: I thought Marie's demonstration was terrific [*uma belezura*], as Paulo Freire would say... simpler than Silvana's.... And Claudia's ...... I'm not sure I understood. What do you guys think? Claudia, can you explain to me better...

(20:31:41) Maria: Yes I understand ACH, but I saw it as a plane and not as a subset of the plane.

(20:31:45) Marie: Maria, we make a great pair. You know all the theorems and I know things from practice, from having worked and tried hard to make geometry "concrete" for my students.

(20:34:33) Carlos: We tried to show that there are two concurrent straight lines in a plane that are parallel to the other plane.

(20:39:59) mborba: Claudia, I understood your demonstration, with Carlos' explanation, and I think it is the simplest! Congratulations! Nice work!

We notice in this excerpt that terms presented in the course of the debate were clarified with the help of other participants. In addition, Marie highlighted distinct approaches to dealing with geometrical problems: mathematical formalization and "practical" work, which we interpret as being exploratory activities with software, manipulative material, etc. In this way, we can identify that the two approaches are complementary, from the perspective of the teacher-students as well as the professors, since it becomes explicit that this activity, in particular, addresses both aspects. We also note that various mathematical argumentations were presented during the debate, and that some were easier to understand than others for some of the participants. Perhaps chat itself, due do its nature, allows various demonstrations and justifications to be presented simultaneously, thus characterizing a transformation in the mathematics produced using chat.

In this chapter, we presented some examples of mathematical problems discussed in chat, and we pointed out that transformations occur in mathematics education when activities that are specific to this field of knowledge are debated in chat sessions. The nature of mathematical discussions in chat is qualitatively different from those that take place via videoconference, and to exemplify this, we present some examples in the following chapter of GPIMEM's experiences with teacher education courses in which the mathematic production is conditioned by another actor, the videoconference, which has unique aspects such as orality and sharing of images.

CHAPTER III

DISTANCE MATHEMATICS EDUCATION USING VIDEOCONFERENCE

In the preceding chapter, we presented examples from our experiences with distance teacher education in which chat was the principal environment for interaction among participants. In this chapter, we will present experiences that differ significantly due to the communication interface used in online distance education: teacher education courses conducted via videoconference. We describe some episodes of mathematical discussion that took place in which problems were resolved collaboratively using this synchronous platform.

THE CONTEXT

In 2001, the Bradesco Foundation acquired the Geometricks software for use in its network of 40 schools located throughout Brazil, with at least one school in each state. It came to their attention after some time, however, that teachers were not incorporating the software into their classes. Foundation members therefore felt it would be pertinent to provide training to teachers to familiarize them with this technological resource.

Two GPIMEM members (and authors of this book) organized a course called Geometry with Geometricks, with the proposal of collectively producing knowledge about geometry (contents), about the use of a given software in the classroom (pedagogical content), and about the use of the software itself (technological).

In light of the unique aspects of this institution, particularly its geographic coverage, the development of a distance course using Internet resources was considered opportune. In addition to the lower cost, actions of this type prevent teachers from having to travel to another location and allows to them to participate and also carry on their classroom work, making it possible for them to put their ideas into practice during the course, thus enriching the exchange of experiences.

The first type of distance course in mathematics offered to the teachers by the Bradesco Foundation was based on a model that involved little interaction between the leader and participants and among participants, similar to the model "virtualization of traditional teaching" mentioned in Chapter I. When we began our course, we had to overcome some initial resistance to our model, which was based on online interaction and applications of Geometricks for elementary and high school levels. Our pedagogical approach included two central points: synchronous interactions among those involved in the course, and the active participation of teacher-students.

Aiming to meet these demands, the technological resources used were varied. The Bradesco Foundation provided access to an Internet environment in which the teacher-students could access the so-called "screens" of the course, which were prepared by the professors and were intended to present the course to the teacher-students, as well as make available the activities to be developed in the course. Below is an example of a screen:

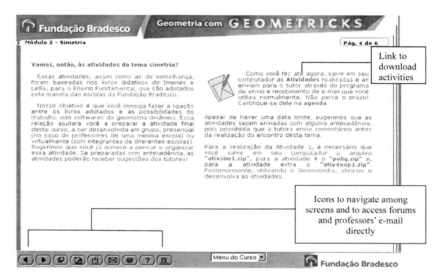

Figure 3

When accessing this environment, the teacher-students were able to use other resources, in addition to reading the assigned texts. Some icons can be seen in the lower part of the screen, for example. Two were for moving forward and backward. Another had a return index, which enabled the user to go directly to a given page. There was also an icon for communicating in the forum, one for chat, and another to send e-mail directly to the professors within the environment.

In addition to this restricted environment, it was possible to use an environment pertaining to the Foundation to conduct videoconferences[1]. This environment also had a specific page, requiring a login and password, which everyone could access from anywhere in the country. It included resources that enabled synchronous communication between the professors and the teacher-students, and as is characteristic of videoconferences, everyone who was connected in the environment was able to hear the person who was speaking.

We noted that the platform also allowed sharing of images[2], as illustrated in FIG. 4, in a way that the image would appear small and could be viewed at the same time another program was being used (Geometricks, Power Point, or any other). We also discovered that, due to limitations of the Internet connection[3], people's images could not be maintained simultaneously with the sharing of Geometricks. Thus, the images were made available at the time of the presentation, and most of the time, participants shared the sound and software screen where the geometric constructions were taking place (FIG. 5).

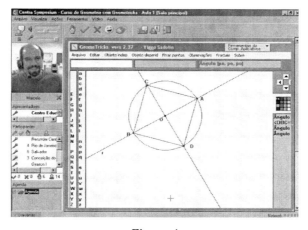

Figure 4

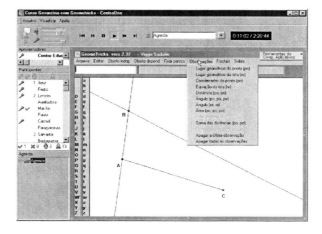

Figure 5

The computer screen of one of the professors was shared, enabling everyone to see the file opened on the computer, which could be in Word, Power Point, or any other program. Geometricks was the program that was used the most, and everyone was able to follow the geometric constructions being made with it.

A rich alternative was discovered during the course: it was possible for any participant to control the mouse of the computer that was sharing Geometricks. In other words, an open file on the professor's computer could be modified by anyone. As this control with the mouse could be compared to a pen, Zulatto and Borba (2006) called this "passing the pen". With this new possibility, students shed their passive roles as observers of geometric constructions and assumed an active role in the process of mathematical production.

Weekly meetings were scheduled to maintain this interaction. For two hours every Saturday, for a period of approximately three months, professors and teacher-students engaged in interaction via videoconference. To put into practice the proposal of active student participation, all the mathematical contents were planned in the form of exploratory problem solving activities. The problems could generally be solved in more than one way, and could be incorporated at different educational levels in accordance with the level of demand regarding the solution and the preference of the teacher-student. Intuitive and formal solutions were both recognized as important, and articulation between trial-and-error and geometric arguments was encouraged.

These activities were developed by the teacher-students and sent to the professors by e-mail (this resource was used considerably for contacts during the asynchronous period during the week) and discussed during the synchronous meetings on Saturdays. They were divided into four themes: familiarization with the software; similarity; symmetry; and analytic geometry. One meeting was dedicated to readings to encourage critical reading regarding the use of informatics in the classroom.

In order for the teacher-students to participate actively, presenting their ideas, sharing solutions to the problems posed, and contributing to the mathematical discussion, it was necessary to limit the number of participants. Therefore, to meet the demand of people interested, three editions of the course were offered in three consecutive semesters, beginning in the second semester of 2004.

Students' evaluations of the course, and especially its effects in the classroom as the Bradesco Foundation teachers incorporated Geometricks into their activities, led to the creation of a new course based on the same participatory proposal as the first. The theme chosen by the teacher-students to study was functions. The software chosen to explore this theme was Winplot, because it is relatively easy to use and free. The course, entitled Functions with Winplot, was offered twice, in the first and second semesters of 2006.

As in the preceding courses, eight synchronous meetings via videoconference were scheduled to explore a set of activities planned around a textbook adopted by the Bradesco Foundation. Two texts on the theme of functions and technology were also assigned and discussed in one of the meetings.

VISUALIZATION IN VIDEOCONFERENCES

In Chapter I, we presented our conception of learning as being related to dialogue, interaction, and collaboration. Communication via chat, videoconference, e-mail, or telephone, for example, differs in various ways, illustrating the role of the medium in the process of knowledge production.

Interfacing with mathematics education, and echoing our previous discussion about unique aspects of chat, Bairral (2004) presents an analysis of the discursive specificities of chat, focusing on the sharing and construction of mathematical knowledge. Based on experiences with mathematics teachers in distance courses on Geometry of short duration which employed synchronous and asynchronous resources, he emphasizes the possibility of joint elaboration of a line of thinking, and observes that, in this environment for interaction, there is an emphasis on written discourse and the need for immediate response, with collaborative reflection. Among the advantages of chat cited by Bairral are the automatic records of the communication and instantaneous exchange of opinions. On the other hand, negative aspects include the need to limit the number of people participating, as it is impossible for many people to follow the discussion, insert images, and draw explanations.

With videoconference, it is possible to explore and share visual images synchronously. It is an alternative in online distance education that can overcome geographical limitations and enable interaction, like other environments such as chat, but which differs due to the possibility of oral dialogue and visualization, although it is still limited to a small number of participants.

According to the National Curriculum Parameters for Mathematics (*Parâmetros Curriculares Nacionais* - PCN, BRAZIL, 1998), mathematical thinking develops initially through visualization. Fonseca et al. (2001, p.75), writing about geometry at the elementary grade level, point out that visualization as approached in the national parameters is restricted to attentive observation of geometric figures, and they argue in favor of adopting a broader meaning that:

> includes the formation or conception of a mental visual image (of something that is not beheld by the eyes at the moment). This is because, in fact, it is in the exercise of observing geometric forms that constitute space, and describing and comparing their differences, that children construct a mental image, which enables them to think about the subject in its absence.

37

In mathematics, visualization is associated with the ability to interpret and understand information presented in the form of figures. However, two processes can occur: interpret a visual image, or create one based on non-figural information. We consider visualization to be a "process of forming images (mentally, with paper and pencil, or with the aid of technology), and using them with the aim of obtaining a better mathematical understanding and stimulating the mathematical discovery process" (ZIMMERMANN AND CUNNINGHAM, 1991, cited in BORBA; VILLARREAL, 2005, p.80)

The act of visualizing can consist of the mental construction of objects, or of processes associated with them, perceived by the individual as external. Alternatively, it can also consist of a construction in an external medium, such as paper-and-pencil, chalkboard, or computer screen, of objects or events that the individual associates with objects or processes in his mind. Nevertheless, despite the distinction between what is external (paper, computer, etc.) and what is internal (mental), it is the individual who perceives (rather than some other person who defines) the objects as internal or external (BORBA; VILLARREAL, 2005).

According to Cifuentes (2005), to visualize is to be able to form mental images, and this lies at the root of the entire process of abstraction. He argues that the visual aspect of mathematics should not be associated with physical perception alone, but also with a mode of intellectual perception related to mathematical intuition. He calls attention to the fact that little emphasis is given in mathematics to intuition and the thinking processes associated with it, such as visualization, narrative and inductive arguments.

From this perspective, computers are not seen as mere aids for mathematicians, but rather as transforming the nature of mathematics itself, and therefore actors in the thinking collective. In the context of mathematics education, visualization is part of the teaching and learning process, of students' mathematical production. As Garnica (1995) suggests, the eyes can be valued as an organ that makes discovery possible. This being so, when we do not have access to external representations identifiable to the eyes, we turn to internal representations constructed in the course of our mathematical experiences.

Therefore, visualization has pedagogical value and is related to students' comprehension, which translates into internal or external representations, with and without the use of media. With technological advances, however, it has become very associated with media, the computer in particular.

Thus, visualization is considered a resource for mathematical comprehension, and the computer can be used to test conjectures, to calculate, and to decide questions that are based on visual information. Lourenço (2002, p.107) believes informatics can contribute to "induce demonstrations" or "aid in the search for results", as well as to "encourage research".

Reflecting on these aspects, while structuring the "Geometry with

Geometricks" and "Functions with Winplot" courses, the software was the technology chosen to enable external visualization, a priori; the videoconference environment provided the opportunity to share the constructions created in that environment, fomenting interaction and dialogue, as the activities were discussed.

MATHEMATICAL PROBLEMS IN VIDEOCONFERENCE

The Case of Geometry

Considering the questions raised and discussed above, we present examples in this section of activities proposed to the teacher-students in the Bradesco Foundation courses. They are based on the experimental-with-technologies approach; in other words, participants were expected to investigate the problems proposed to them with the aid of technological resources. It is important to emphasize that all of the teacher-students participated throughout the course, speaking, listening, and manipulating software. As an illustration, we present excerpts from an activity[4] that addressed questions of symmetry, beginning with the statement:

FINDING THE SYMMETRIES

a) If necessary, review what is axial symmetry.

b) Using the file "ativsim1.tri", find the symmetric figures in relation to the x and y axes given.

The figures sent in the file "ativsim1" were:

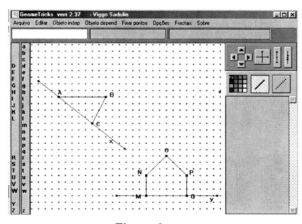

Figure 6

A file was made available, in the environment of the course, to all the teacher-students containing a figure MNOPQ (FIG.7) and asking them to find the figure symmetric to it in relation to the "q" axis. We observed in the statement that symmetry should be maintained even if the vertices were dragged on the screen.

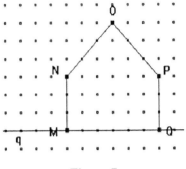

Figure 7

The activities developed by the teacher-students were sent to the course professors prior to the synchronous meeting, making it possible to plan the class to take advantage of their errors. Questions were raised that allowed participants to perceive what their mistakes were and why they made them, and the "correct" answers were presented by their colleagues, without referring directly to those who made the mistakes if possible. In this way, knowledge could be produced collectively without exposing the participants in the course.

The majority sent in the activity having used the Cartesian plane to find the symmetrical points, counting the distance from the points to the axis and marking the points below it with the same distance in relation to q. The visual result is presented in FIG.8:

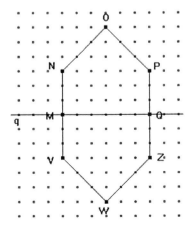

Figure 8

A volunteer was chosen to "command the pen", and this construction was carried out in the synchronous meeting guided by another volunteer who was in charge of speaking, like a sportscaster. Questions arose in the course of the construction, such as: Is MVWZQ symmetric to MNOPQ? Why? The discussions were inevitable. Some of the manifestations were affirmative, which generated observations regarding the possibility of "dragging", observing that if the vertex were dragged, the symmetry between the figures would be lost (FIG.9).

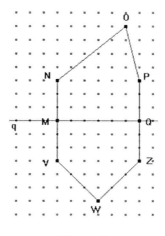

Figure 9

Few observed that the problem statement itself had called attention to this fact, and they were asked how a construction could be made that would resist dragging. Some theoretical aspects were also addressed, justifying the search for a solution that resisted dragging. For Laborde (1998) and Olivero *et al.* (1998), and other researchers on this theme, a quadrilateral, for example, with four equal sides and four right angles is only considered a square in dynamic geometry software if it passes the "dragging test", i.e., if when one of its vertices is dragged, it still has four equal sides and angles, maintaining its properties. If not, rather than saying a square has been constructed ("robust construction"), we say a square has been drawn ("soft construction").

Some suggestions were verbalized in the attempt to find the figure symmetric to MNOPQ that would pass the "drag test". A volunteer accepted the challenge and requested the "pen" to make a construction. The concepts used in the previous activity were remembered and associated with the figure, and using circumferences (center in M and in Q and radiuses MN, MO, MP, QP, QO, QN), performing the role of compass, and perpendicular to the axis, passing through points N, O, and P (which do not belong to the axis), the symmetric figure MVWZQ was found which maintained its symmetry to MNOPQ even when one of its vertices was dragged (FIG.10).

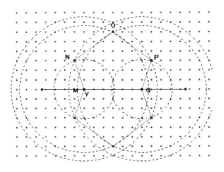

Figure 10

Another example highlights the interaction, in this case, between professor and student, which took place in the exploration of an activity about similarity. The assigned activity was:

INITIAL EXPLORATION

1) Construct a quadrilateral ABCD with the
following angles:
= 100° ; = 70° ; = 80° ; = 110°

2) Construct a figure similar to the first one.

After presenting the activity, it was asked if someone would like to develop it. André "asked for the pen" and began to draw the construction. He marked two points, A and B, and joined them with a segment. He then drew a line through A at a 100° angle to segment AB. Next, he inserted a second line that passed through B, forming a 70° angle with AB. To do this, he used the command "Angle (point, line, measure)", which requires clicking on: the point where you want to construct a line; the line or segment where the desired angle is to be formed; and the measure of the angle between the two lines. In this case, for example, he first clicked on point A, then on segment AB, and then typed the measure 100°. Since the software always considers the angle in a counter-clockwise manner, to mark the line that passes through B forming a 70° angle with AB, it is necessary to type the measure of its supplementary angel, 110° (FIG.11).

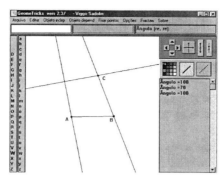

Figure 11

When André went to do the same with point C, to find the angle = 80° in ABCD, he clicked first on point C and then on the line passing through B and C. When he checked to see if he had followed the correct procedure, he was surprised to see "100°". His reaction and the professor's response in the excerpt that follows illustrate the collective nature of the work that took place in the synchronous meetings:

> André: Let's just check to see if the angle is 80 degrees. Let's go to 'observations'..., 'angle (line, line)"..., in a counter-clockwise direction..., first line, OK!, second... 100 degrees? I think we did something wrong. Marcelo, help please!
>
> Marcelo: Let's do this little part here, answering André's call for help... (laughing). But this here is great... so let's go here... 'erase last object', and go here 'dependent object', 'angle (point, line, measure)'. So... point, line, and ... here now we'll see the following, we are going counter-clockwise... So if we put here, intuition tells us to put a 100 degree angle here to make it 80, let's test the hypothesis... So, and we get out... because it is counter-clockwise and it's considering that line, that point, so we did it where the cursor is passing the 100 degree angle, which means that the internal angle will be 80. That was the only detail that our colleagues from São Luis forgot. But Rubia and I are amazed, not only because you guys are doing it, but because the way Rubia and I had thought about doing it was not as efficient as this way. So the way the colleagues from São Luis are doing it is better than the way Rubia and I had thought about it and had done it – last year and this year - while preparing for the class.

In this excerpt, one can note the interaction between student and professor collaborating to draw the construction requested by the activity. André's error did not discredit the solution. On the contrary, the possibility of sharing solutions with the software enriched the exchange among participants, and in this case, his solution was more appropriate than the one the professors had thought of, and merited recognition.

A second example we feel is interesting illustrates the investigative approach of the course. The activities were developed in such a way as to stimulate students to find justifications for their answers. They were open activities which, while perhaps having a single solution, could usually be solved by following different paths. Many of the teacher-students knew how to use mathematical properties to develop the activities, but were not able to justify them. Hypotheses and conjectures were raised during the activities that were not accompanied by explanations.

When the justifications and argumentations were not explored in the synchronous meetings, they were developed asynchronously and shared, enabling the exchange of ideas between teacher-students and professors during the week. In their teaching practice, few of the teachers felt the need to seek mathematical justifications for conclusions obtained, and they were therefore not familiar with this type of proposal. Together, they were able to avail themselves of mutual help, or even appropriate a solution presented by a colleague. On occasion, it was even suggested that the teacher-students attempt to carry out a formal demonstration of the problem in question. As an example, we present an activity aimed at exploring the bisectrices of a parallelogram, as proposed below:

EXPLORING BISECTRICES OF A PARALLELOGRAM

1. Construct a parallelogram ABCD
2. Draw the bisectrices of the internal angles of the parallelogram
3. The four bisectrices form a quadrilateral EFGH
4. What can you say about the quadrilateral EFGH?
5. What happens when you drag points A, B, C or D?
6. What conditions are necessary for the quadrilateral EFGH to be a square?
7. What quadrilateral do you obtain when you draw the bisectrices of the quadrilateral EFGH? Justify your answer.
8. What happens if ABCD is a square? Why?

After reading the activity and constructing items 1 to 3, the teacher-students were questioned about the quadrilateral EFGH (question 4).

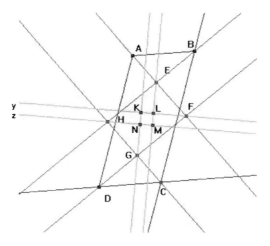

Figure 12

Elaine stated that EFGH was a parallelogram, after which Artur proposed that it was a rectangle. Neuza shared his opinion. Marcelo, as professor, tried to pose questions to encourage reflection and seek justifications, taking advantage of the teacher-students' suggestions. Initially he asked if all rectangles are parallelograms. Pedro observed that, to answer this, one needed only to check to see if the measurements of the angles were 90° using the software menu. This was done, the measurements were confirmed, and it was clarified, as in most books, that a rectangle is a specific case of parallelogram; however a mathematical explanation to justify the measurements of the angles was lacking.

> Marcelo: The problem is that, in addition to the measurement of the angles done by Geometricks, if we can use a demonstration to introduce seventh or eighth grade students that we are doing this construction of bisectrices like this, for example, on the chalkboard, or even with Geometricks, that we will have a rectangle inside there. Was anyone able to do that? Or, if no one was able to do it, we will open a forum to try; we'll put this question about a demonstration in the forum. Rubia and I will show the first step, give a clue, in case no one presents the beginning of the demonstration, or - who knows? - maybe the whole demonstration by Monday, OK?!

In addition to justifying that EFGH is a rectangle, we were seeking arguments for Pedro's hypothesis: "One thing we observed, too, is that when you draw the bisectrices of the rectangle, you will have a square in the center of the rectangle". The excerpts that follow illustrate the participation of the teacher-students.

> Lincoln: Professor, one thing we observe is that if you take the bisectrix

that passes through vertex E, its intersection with the side that follows our rectangle forms there, if we could measure the side EF and if F goes to the point of the intersection and we discover that it has two equal sides, then we can see that the intersection will determine the side of a square, consecutive equal sides, of you could mark the intersection on the bisectrix that passes through vertex E and intersects with side FG, we could see that it appears to form a square EF and F at the intersection. The angle, and since it is a bisectrix, if the angle is 90°, we get 45°. And we can also see that the triangle ELF is an isosceles triangle, because its sides are equal? If we could prove this relation between the figures until we get to the angle of the square, or as we said, square, we are trying to prove the thesis that it is a square or not.

Marcelo: Look, Lincoln's idea is very interesting. Analyzing triangle ELF is a triangle that will have its internal angles, angle E will measure 45°, since it is a bisectrix of the rectangle. The internal angle of this triangle that has two blue sides and one red, angle F will also have 45°, and therefore angle L will have 90°. So this is an isosceles triangle. And so what do we do to conclude this reasoning that KLMN is a square?

Lincoln was engaged in the problem and continued:

Lincoln: So what I said is true, but even so, arriving at the conclusion that K, L, and M are right angles, can we still affirm that it is a square? Because what is left to do is measure these distances, right? KL, LM, MN, and NK, equal distances, i.e. the sides maintaining, the congruent sides, same value, we can conclude that it would therefore be a square, or is what I'm saying not true?

The challenge, at this point, was to find a justification for equal measurements for the sides KLMN. Maria Divina initiated this part and the debate continued until our time ran out:

Maria Divina: I was observing bisectrix E that passes the distance from bisectrix G, and if you observe bisectrix F also passes the same distance from bisectrix H. [...] If the four parallels, the perpendiculars, we can observe this question there of the parallelism and perpendicularism. You can really know that the distance is the same.

Marcelo: Maria, I think there is an argument missing. It is already clear that the angles are 90°, therefore the blue lines are parallel, i.e. y is parallel to z, OK? And x is parallel to w. But how can I conclude from that that KL is therefore parallel to MN, but how am I going to from that ... Since the angles are equal, I can say KL is congruent with MN, but how can we say KL is congruent with KN? This is the question left to resolve. Once this is resolved, if KL is congruent to KN, we follow a similar reasoning to say that KL is congruent to LM, actually, we don't even need to, because since they are parallel, the issue is solved. Does anyone have a suggestion?

Pedro: The idea would be to think, like, if we have a triangle ELF, putting a segment EL and we have a segment a little bigger on the same line EM. The subtraction of these segments EM – LE gives the segment of the square, that is, which is the thesis we are trying to prove, that it is a square. In the same way, we get point H, where the bisectrix of this vertex is, measure the distance HM, HN, subtract these two distances, since I know that these segments NH and LE are practically congruent, they have the same value, then I can conclude that MN and LN have the same measure, we can arrive at the conclusion that it really is a square, correct?

Marcelo: Pedro, this is one of the difficulties of doing geometry over distance, but it doesn't seem to me, if I was able to follow your steps, I don't think there was a conclusion about this yet (Long Pause).

Rúbia: Lincoln, if I understood your comments, if what you said is valid, it is resolved, because LM will be equal to MN. My doubt now is, how are you guaranteeing that EM is exactly equal to HN, and then, why did you say NH is equal to EL, OK?! (Long Pause)

Marcelo: People, we are running out of time and this question will remain open here now. Of course measuring the angles in the way that was proposed we would see, and measuring the segments, we would see that it was a square. The question then that remains open is still to prove that KLMN is a square – we're getting there! But it's no problem, and this demonstration could be omitted when working with fifth to eighth grade students; they can simply experience that it is a square, but maybe it would be possible to do this at the high school level, OK?!

The discussion of this activity extended to a collective interaction that went beyond the synchronous meetings, with demonstrations being elaborated and shared by e-mail.

With this example, one can see that the teacher-students raised hypotheses and sought to justify them, exploring the quadrilateral EFGH formed by the bisectrices of the original figure ABCD and the quadrilateral KLMN formed by the bisectrices of EFGH. The ideas and arguments were shared collectively as they arose. The synchronous meeting enabled simultaneous dialogue and interaction among everyone involved in the process of knowledge production.

This activity also illustrates how conjectures were often raised by the students themselves (they were the ones who concluded that EFGH was a rectangle and KLMN was a square) and how the arguments were developed collectively. There was an exchange of knowledge among the colleagues, who sought to form arguments, albeit informal, regarding the properties involved. The ideas were being shared through dialogue, and different possibilities were highlighted. The thinking was collective in a learning process that involved propositions and "mathematical argumentations". This is usually an individual activity, each with their own book, paper, and pencil, in most of our face-to-face and distance education experiences. Professors present some demonstrations, explain the process of arguments, and invite students to try to develop them. Supported by results, propositions, etc., we demonstrate theorems thinking with paper, pencil, and books. This is the usual practice in mathematics classes.

The course allowed space for a new way; demonstration occurred collaboratively in an online environment. The arguments were not presented or elaborated by one person but rather constructed based on contributions from different participants. It was not possible to identify "the author" of this process, and the participants thought with Geometricks, with their colleagues, and each may have even had in hand paper and pencil.

Following this sequence of justifications was not easy, despite being able to visualize the figures on the computer screen. Perhaps because it is a practice that differs from the one we are accustomed to, it was difficult to follow the different lines of reasoning that emerged and were not always completed. In real time, it was possible to follow the reasoning of the students, which did not necessarily follow a logical sequence. With orality, linearity – which is "common" in writing, for example – is often lacking. Each person shared their reasoning with the others, which often required effort to follow and organize.

The Case of Functions

In this section, we present an example in which two software programs were used in the course "Functions with Winplot". This example illustrates how a teacher-student appropriated Geometricks after having used it in the "Geometry with Geometricks" course, proposing a solution that integrated it with Winplot, in the group that participated in the course in the second semester of 2006.

Considering that the course was developed for mathematics professors, one could say that the proposal of the activity was simple:

ACTIVITY

Construct graphs of the functions $y = x$, $y = 2x$ and $y = 2x + 1$. Point out similarities and differences between these functions, regarding aspects such as domain, image, roots, slope, etc.

This was the first activity that the teacher-students had to develop by themselves and send the solution prior to the meeting where it would be discussed. The objective was to begin to familiarize them with Winplot using contents frequently addressed in the classroom. During the videoconference, with "pen in hand", Alessandro constructed the three functions:

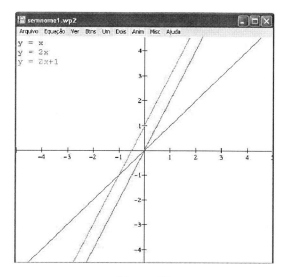

Figure 13

Analyzing the similarities and differences, Neuza pointed out that the function y=x is the identity, and that graphically, this line "crosses" the first and third quadrants. She also observed that it forms a 45° angle with the X axis, and that its angular coefficient is 1. Regarding the function y=2x, she stated that its angular coefficient is 2, with a straight slope of approximately 63°, like the function y=2x+1, which was moved to the left, with the two being parallel to each other.

The professor asked how she had arrived at this value of 63°. Neuza clarified that she had used Geometricks. She had opened the software to find the solution she presented. The function y=2x+1 was constructed:

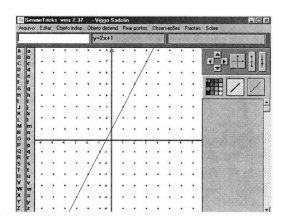

Figure 14

However, since Geometricks does not consider the intersection of the axes with the line constructed, it was necessary to draw a line on the X axis in order to calculate the value of the angle. At this moment, others began to participate actively, offering suggestions of other possibilities. Waldemir suggested that two points be created on the X axis and that a line then be drawn passing through them. The professor asked if there was not an easier alternative, and Adeilton suggested drawing the function y=0. With the lines drawn, it was possible to find the value of the angle using the resources of the software: 63.44°.

The professor called attention to the fact that Neuza was already thinking using Geometricks, considering that she had used it to find the value of the angle of the incline of the line, even though the course had been planned around the use of Winplot. He also observed that, when Neuza presented her idea, she thought about the possibility of calculating the angle based on a rectangular triangle, and asked the teacher-students how this process would be carried out.

Adeilton suggested using the tangent of the angle, and the professor responded with another question: How could one use the tangent of an angle without knowing its measurement? Adeilton then suggested analyzing the rectangular triangle (FIG.15, represented here to highlight it) with the coordinates (2,1), (0,1) and (0,5).

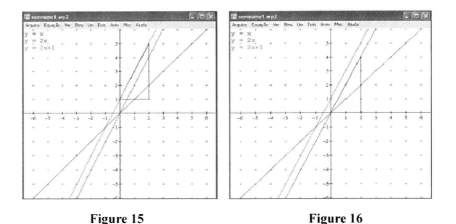

Figure 15   Figure 16

The professor agreed, and commented that he had in mind the triangle with the coordinates (2,4), (2,0) and (0,0), as illustrated in FIG.16. He explained that, in this way, they would be considering the function y=2x, and not y=2x+1, but as Neuza had explained, the angle of the incline of the two lines was the same. Since the tangent is defined as the ratio of the measures of the opposite cathetus and the adjacent cathetus, it was possible to see that the tangent of the angle we were seeking was 2.

The question that remained to be answered, then, was: What function should be used to find the angle, if it was known that its tangent had a value of 2? José Ivan suggested using a calculator, and Adeilton complemented this with the indication that the function to be requested on the calculator should be the arctangent.

This situation elucidates how people can think differently, depending on the availability of different media. Since the objective of the course was to explore the theme of functions and familiarize the teacher-students with Winplot, the activities had been planned using this medium. It would thus seem natural to try to resolve the problem using this software.

However, what we noticed was that, following the Geometry course, Neuza had begun using Geometricks often (she had reported using it constantly in her classes) and thinking with it. It had become natural for her to turn to this medium to solve the problem.

The professor of the course had, in the past, used the calculator as the principal technological resource in his classes. When he thought about confirming whether or not Neuza's answer was correct, he immediately began thinking about the best path to take using this medium.

Although the numerical solutions found were the same – approximately 63° - the paths taken and mathematical concepts addressed were different. And, as the participants shared their solutions in a collective environment, it was possible for them to visualize all the alternatives, and even complement those presented by their colleagues.

ONLINE DISTANCE EDUCATION IN ACTION

The examples presented here illustrate how videoconference provided the opportunity for a construction to be initiated by a teacher-student and continued by the professor or another teacher-student in a collaborative process. Other examples like these took place during the courses. The participants evaluated positively the possibility of solving problems in a collective manner during the synchronous sessions, despite the slow pace of this type of pedagogical proposal, as technical issues slowed the construction down, and also the pace of the teacher-students differed from that of the professors because they were less familiar with the platform and the activities. This can be observed in the comment of one of the participants:

> André: We also have a positive evaluation. This business of passing the pen to others appears to slow things down, but it ends up being very interesting. You can see each person's difficulties. It's extremely positive. (2nd edition of the "Geometry with Geometricks" course, first semester, 2005)

The opinions expressed by the teacher-students also emphasize the exchange that took place based not only on the professors' experiences, but also those of their colleagues, with collaboration being encouraged by the possibility of "passing the pen":

> Marcos: [...] dynamism of the class happens, where the pen is given, that's exactly when situations come up that weren't even expected by you guys [professors], and our colleagues raise this situations, and it's also easy for us, on the other hand, to understand much better. And I want to say, then, that I resolved many of my own doubts this way, and I started to have a much better understanding than before. (first edition of the "Functions with Winplot" course, first semester, 2006)

> Neuza: The class was really productive for us [...], and we were able to resolve our doubts during the explanations - of Prof. Marcelo, of Prof.Rúbia, and also of our colleagues in the other schools of the Foundation. (second edition of the "Functions with Winplot" course, second semester, 2006)

The teacher-students also emphasized that the collaboration in the collective construction was more interesting than the constructions which they merely observed as "telespectators" of a single solution presented by the professors, even when the solution had been sent by one of them. We believe that this virtual collaboration created a link that was not experienced when these technical resources were not used. The discussion about "construction versus drawing" is not new in the literature, but we believe that our experience with it in a distance course is original, born of the collaboration between professors and students.

The examples presented in this chapter illustrate the role of media in the process of knowledge production. With the resources of videoconference, the collaboration was qualitatively different from the collaboration we experienced using chat. Also different was the way of thinking about the same activity using the different technologies available – the different software programs and the calculator. This is a theme we will develop in greater depth in the next chapter.

CHAPTER IV

HUMANS-WITH-INTERNET

In Borba and Penteado (2001), the non-secondary role of computers in the way knowledge is produced was discussed. Paper and pencil shape the way a mathematical demonstration is done; orality plays an analogous role as an idea matures; and graphing software, or any electronic spreadsheet that generates tables and graphs, can transform the way a given subject or specific topic, in the context of mathematics, for example, is addressed.

As an illustration, we can highlight the work of Benedetti (2003), who, with the use of a graphing software program, was able to get 8th grade students to elaborate conjectures about functions. Studies like this one, and others like Scucuglia (2006), Accioli (2005), and Borba (1993), illustrate how the presence of a software program or a graphing calculator significantly modifies the way knowledge is produced in educational environments. Malheiros (2004) discusses how software programs participate actively in the elaboration and solution of open problems developed by students, broadening and adding new layers to the studies of Borba et al. (1999a, 1999b) within the trend in mathematics education called modeling[1].

Common to these studies, and to a large universe of other studies, is the fact that the student is not only listening to the teachers, or writing a solution to an exercise, or demonstrating a result. He does these activities, as well, but they are preceded by experimentation aided by technology, almost as a student would do an experiment in a natural sciences class. In some cases, the activities are also followed by verifications or elaboration of new problems in which computers participate, as well.

The continual analysis of examples like these, which began in Borba (1993), as well as the interpretation and adaptation of ideas by authors such as Lévy (1993) and Tikhomirov (1981), led to the idea that software programs are co-authors in the production of knowledge, which we then came to see as produced by humans together with technological interfaces. In this sense, the discussion of software design and ways than humans interact with computers was no longer an object of study only for the fields of computer science or HCI[2], but for (mathematics) education, as well.

The perception of the relevance of the participation of computer technologies in the educational context generated the idea that thinking is reorganized by a given technology and that mathematical knowledge is generated by collectives of humans and non-humans. These ideas, originally published in Borba (1994; 1996; 1999a), have been developed since the 1990s to account for the perception that not only do computer technologies shape the production of knowledge, but so do orality and writing, as proposed by Borba (1993). Influenced by Lévy's and Tikhomirov's discussions of the relation between technology and humans, these ideas were broadened and synthesized in Borba and Villarreal (2005), who, based on a large set of studies, argue that knowledge is produced by collectives of humans-with-media. Humans are fundamental to the production of knowledge, and so is the medium. This construct suggests the need for a means of expression, a medium, to produce knowledge. In this sense, Borba argues that "knowledge, which is seen here as being strongly influenced by the media being used, is not only influenced by the way it is expressed, but is shaped by this media" (2002, p.150).

In this view, mathematical demonstration is a product of humans, but also of paper and pencils, and will be transformed by computer technologies if they continue to spread uncontrollably to all aspects of human life and the world. In a more intense manner, speech is already being changed by the growing mediation of computer technologies, as in the case of videoconference, in which it is necessary to speak more slowly, for example. This perspective of knowledge production implies that it is always undergoing transformation thanks to changes in humans and in media. It is this perspective that has permeated the work of our research group, GPIMEM. This view seems to be echoed by other authors such as Toschi and Rodrigues (2003), who argue that technologies are human creations, but are impregnated with information, thus assuming a cultural dimension. In our view, technologies, and information technologies in particular, are impregnated with humanity, and this can be seen in the way we like or dislike the interface of a give software. It is for this reason that we do not emphasize the humans-versus-technology dichotomy, and argue that knowledge can be seen as the product of collectives of humans-with-media.

Over the past four years, influenced by these ideas and by our eight years of experience with online distance education, we have raised various questions: "Is it possible to apply the construct humans-with-media in the context of online distance education, as well?" or "Does the Internet transform the way mathematics is produced in online courses?"

We have been working on the first response regarding the possibility that Internet may transform mathematics since we first began conducting research in this area. Initially, we sought, in our online practices, something similar to what graphing software brought to the study of functions, i.e., changes in the nature of the production of mathematical knowledge based on unique characteristics like experimentation and visualization.

Thus, in our first studies in online distance courses which involved the use of chat rooms, as presented in Chapter II, concepts arose related to multilogue. In the normal classroom, social norms dictate that only one person speak at a time so that dialogue can be established and learning is possible. In environments with chat, however, while one person is typing, another may be doing the same. A given question may thus generate three "simultaneous" responses. These quotation marks refer to the fact that, while they were generated at the same time, without the respondents being aware of the other responses, they appear in a linear fashion in the chat window. There are numerous examples from our research of how this can generate, exponentially, multiple discussions, and as a result, the professor is unable to maintain the same level of control he or she may have in a traditional classroom. Again, we intend not to analyze whether this is good or not, but only to point out that situations like this occur often in courses that rely heavily on chat. There are those who believe this to be a true "Tower of Babel", to use the expression of one participant in the Trends in Mathematics course in 2000, and which we still hear today. Other participants enjoy having the right to "speak" (write) at the moment they feel like it, without having to ask permission, and yet others complain that the professor only interacts with a limited "part" of the Tower. Sacramento (2006) has pointed out that this requires new abilities of the professor, who has to interact with various themes and students at the same time

It has also been conjectured, but not researched, as far as we know, that each participant has different learning styles, and that some adapt more to the traditional classroom or to online environments in which chat has a predominant role. It may be that people who are timid in face-to-face situations become "talkative" online, and that some prefer presenting their ideas using the Internet as the medium while others prefer to interface only with the air circulating in the classroom. We have also observed that the inability to type can shape the personality of participants in this type of course, and the lack of broad band Internet can also have this effect. Thus, in online environments, we see that interfaces shape our way of being and can attribute new importance to abilities like typing which are not very important in most face-to-face classrooms. The idea of humans-with-media could possibly be extended to this area, and analogous to what happened with mathematics, ICTs could contribute to discovering roles for orality and writing that were hidden in our analyses of normal classrooms. Research based on this theoretical construct will be necessary to solidify the conjectures raised in this paragraph.

On the other hand, there are studies that suggest that the topic under discussion itself shapes the nature of interaction that takes place in environments such as chat rooms. The virtual environment is impregnated with social aspects generated inside and outside of it. We noted, in the version of the Trends course mentioned in Chapter II, in which students explored a spatial geometry activity, that when the discussion focused on mathematical problems rather than the themes we were accustomed to addressing – trends in mathematics education – fewer open discussions occurred. The multilogue was still present, but in a different way, more focused on finding the solution to a problem. It appears that experiences outside the classroom, in which mathematics always has a single answer and is a symbol of certainty (BORBA; SKOVSMOSE, 2001), also invade our new teaching experiences in environments like the ones we are discussing here. Thus, online education, despite being virtual, is conditioned by social factors; in fact, the process through which media shape our cognition is historical, social, and cultural, to the degree that orality, writing, and ICTs are also products with historical, social, and cultural influences. Our observations regarding the different nature of the multilogue that occurred in the chat sessions when mathematical problems were being discussed compared to when trends in mathematics education, like ethnomathematics or mathematical modeling, were being discussed, reflect such influences.

Within this view, computer interfaces, contents, teachers, and students influence the knowledge produced. It is in this sense that the construct humans-with-media is impregnated with social aspects. Knowledge is constructed collectively based on our interactions. The cognitive being does not have limits similar to the biological being. In our research, we have focused on how humans, as they interact with different media, produce knowledge. The use of software programs has conditioned the way visualization and experimentation occur, with characteristics associated with these interfaces. When we look at chat, a characteristic that stands out is the fact that the native written language is the natural vehicle for expression, realizing a perhaps even closer approximation between mathematical and native language than the one proposed by Machado (2001). In the chat room, writing is the only form of communication, of being social. This is what differentiates the writing that characterizes a virtual chat from face-to-face chat, in which orality and gestures occupy spaces that must be filled by the written word in online chat environments.

In this sense, the Internet conditions the way we know, as illustrated with examples in preceding chapters. It is based on this perspective that we state that humans-with-Internet produce knowledge via chat. And within the humans-with-Internet collective, further distinctions could be made between "with-chat" or "with-videoconference". Other experiences we have had, as reported in Chapter III, have led us to see how videoconference is a form of orality. In this virtual orality, the acceptable social norms change somewhat, and in many respects, are similar to those in a normal classroom, i.e. speaking one at a time, although parallel conversations may be legitimate in locales other than the "stage" of the videoconference without violating etiquette.

The possibility of visualizing in a shared and synchronous manner with Geometricks and Winplot in videoconference shapes the actions in the same way that "passing the pen" represents a qualitatively different possibility for collaboration which is not always naturally possible in face-to-face environments. Synchronous image and sound make collaboration more fair and equal. As Lévy (1993) observed, the use of chat or videoconference in our courses did not exclude the use of other media like paper-and-pencil, which were used by everyone individually.

In this scenario, it is relevant to ask: What importance can dialogue have in learning? As we have already stated, we believe there is a relation between the quality of the dialogue and the quality of the mathematical learning. How and with whom we speak opens up different possibilities for learning. Videoconference provided an environment for interaction via oriality, which is the usual form of everyday communication. It is via orality that we are accustomed to exchanging ideas, whereas mathematical expression via writing alone, as occurs with chat, for example, requires another way of thinking, of expressing ideas and reasoning that are developed in the course of the activity, in a multilogue. There is no need to compare them or define which is the better resource.

In both online distance education experiences of GPIMEM (the "Trends in Mathematics Education" courses and the courses carried out in partnership with the Bradesco Foundation), language played a crucial role, written as well as spoken. The possibility of hearing the teacher-students explain their ideas and present their solutions to the activities proposed during the videoconferences orally and visually, and the discussions via chat which allowed them to make their points freely without waiting their turn, or even to comment on different subjects at the same time, made the courses environments for collaborative production of knowledge. It is this collaborative work that distinguishes these experiences from most existing online distance education, particularly in the field of mathematics. The examples presented point to the ways the different ICT interfaces influence the production of knowledge by collectives of humans-with-media.

THE STUDENT AND THE MEDIA IN ONLINE DISTANCE EDUCATION

In online distance education, students assume a different role, and it is important that they adapt to new situations that emerge in this educational modality, as the student is normally responsible for organizing their own time and carrying out activities according to their possibilities.

Palloff and Pratt (2002) discuss students' roles in distance courses and note that they are interwoven and interdependent. Thus, students need to be concerned about their knowledge production; act collaboratively, to contribute to collaborative learning; and pay attention to the management of the learning process, managing their time, developing the assigned activities, etc. It is hoped that they will learn to learn, and acquire the capacity to think critically.

Thus, just as the teacher experiences changes in their role, which we will address in the next section, students also have to rethink their way of acting in the teaching and learning process, as they need to know how to manage their time. This tends to be the greatest challenge for students, as traditionally the time is defined and fixed. As the time becomes more flexible, online distance education requires self control and discipline on the part of the student, since flexibility does not imply decreased amount of time dedicated to the activities.

In addition to considering these aspects of the student's role in online distance education, we ask: What about the media? Is it possible that they condition the way students act in this modality of teaching and learning? We believe they do. For many people, for example, participation in their first chat session coincides with their first class in an online distance course. And how to cope with this? Multilogue, described previously, turns into a Tower of Babel for some, especially those are expecting a virtual environment that imitates the traditional classroom as we know it, as Borba observed (2004). One possibility that we glimpsed and also practiced was to avoid enforcing "rules" and presenting many instructions at the beginning of the courses. In this way, as they participate in the chat sessions, students gradually become familiar with the communication process, and consequently, with online distance education. We often read on the computer screen in the initial meetings phrases like "I'm lost" or "what are you talking about?', and the frequency decreases as the course progresses, as students perceive that that is the "natural" process of the discussion.

Participants' familiarization with the interfaces used is also conditioned by the nature of the discussions. In the Trends course, most of the debates revolve around educational aspects of the theme of the meeting, and multilogue is constant. In the case of mathematical problems, we noticed that students have other types of difficulties, such as visualization or manipulation of a geometric construction, and that when using chat, for example, this only occurs through the coordination of various media, as we illustrated in Chapter II.

Videoconference also conditions the students' role in teaching and learning processes, as they use orality but in a different way than in the usual classroom. In our online meetings, each person speaks one at a time, as individuals request permission to speak and take turns as the class unfolds. The attention students must pay to the words spoken by the others in videoconference also differs from chat, for example, where one can refer to what has already been said by consulting the typed communication that remains recorded and available throughout the class. In this sense, the student's approach tends to be different, and consequently, the teaching and learning process, as well.

Another point we emphasize regarding the role of students and videoconference is related to the coordination of speaking with the use of the software. In the examples we presented, the student often spoke at the same time he constructed a given geometric figure. This aspect shows us that different abilities are important for online distance education using videoconference.

In the face of all this, students' creativity comes to the fore to get around certain situations. They use their imagination to make themselves understood, as in the example presented in Chapter II, when the student compared the physical space of the classroom to a figure being discussed, so that others would perceive that the ceiling and floor were parallel, and from there, continued the mathematical demonstration. Another example that will be discussed in the following chapter involves a student who photographed a graph she had drawn in a sheet of paper and "posted" it in the virtual environment in order for us to visualize it. In the videoconference, it was necessary to be creative when technical problems made it difficult to talk and move the figure constructed with the software, so we began asking one student to describe the construction orally, like a sportscaster, while another developed it. This was one of the alternatives we found to overcome technical problems that arose.

Another aspect that deserves to be mentioned is the completion of assigned activities within established deadlines. Many meetings in online distance education are based on material handed in electronically by the students beforehand, as we have mentioned elsewhere in this book. Activities developed asynchronously are discussed during the synchronous meetings. In order for the student to participate actively, it is important that they be aware of their position, which is not merely recipient of information, but participant in the entire process of teaching and learning. Their role is fundamental for this process to take place, and for this, there must be dedication, which must be encouraged through interaction, collaboration, and dialogue among the actors involved, students and teachers.

THE TEACHER AND THE MEDIA IN ONLINE DISTANCE EDUCATION

Based on our teaching practice and studies in online distance education, we have identified some characteristics of the role of the teacher in these contexts. In chat, for example, certain abilities are important for the class to progress in a satisfactory manner, such as rapid typing and the ability to deal with various questions at the same time – multilogue. Various questions are presented almost simultaneously, and it is up to the teacher to respond to them. Toward this end, some strategies help to guarantee that no questions go unanswered, such as not activating the automatic scroll during chat sessions and instead navigating on the screen using the scroll bar. In addition, it is also important to cite, at the beginning of the answer, the time a given subject or question was raised, as well as type the name of the person who raised it. These are some of the strategies we have used during chat sessions to facilitate and follow the students throughout the virtual meeting.

In classes where the central theme of discussion involved mathematical activities, it was often necessary to coordinate interfaces such as chat and portfolio, or chat and software programs such as Winplot, as illustrated in Chapter II. In order for the teacher to avoid getting lost, it is important, in addition to having prepared the class well, to have all the material sent by the students in hand. It is common for students to present their solutions using tools available in the virtual environment before the online meeting, and analyzing these solutions beforehand can improve the teacher's performance significantly.

We have described some of the specifics that teachers should be attentive to when working with chat. But what about videoconference? Are there abilities specific to this interface? Based on the principle that media condition the production of knowledge, we highlighted orality as being the main actor in the teaching and learning process when videoconference is the medium being used. However, videoconference is also full of particularities, and the teacher must therefore program herself with respect to what she will say and how she will say it, filtering what is considered truly important at that moment. Speech should be slow so that everyone can understand what is being said. In addition, when constructing a figure in Geometricks, for example, the teacher should concentrate, because the chance of "live" error is great.

In virtual learning environments, the role of the teacher undergoes a transformation, as she will develop new activities and interact in different ways compared to the face-to-face class.

In all of our experiences, more than one professor was involved acting at different levels, albeit together, during the courses. The first author of this book was responsible for leading the synchronous classes in all the courses, and there was always at least one more professor who helped with the debates and assumed responsibility for some specific classes, as in the example of Spatial Geometry presented in Chapter II. In addition, the second professor also developed most of the asynchronous interactions in the courses, such as responding to e-mail, for example. Technicians were always present during the sessions, which we consider fundamental to the proper functioning of the classes.

Thus, different interfaces require distinct strategies as well as qualities on the part of the teacher. We believe it is necessary to observe these issues as new interfaces are introduced. For example, we are currently working in a virtual learning environment, TIDIA-Ae that includes hypertext, which enables asynchronous, collective writing, as will be discussed in the following chapter. However, this tool will demand additional care on the part of teachers should they decide to interact directly in a hypertext developed by a group of students. This is a question that has not yet been investigated, but that we are attentive to, as we are aware of the active participation of media in the production of knowledge. This is another illustration of the relevance of the construct humans-with-media: when the role of the media is emphasized, this theoretical construct specifies actions of the teacher who is part of a collective of humans-with-media, calling our attention to the changes introduced into the collective with the participation of new interfaces.

CHAPTER V

MODELING AND ONLINE DISTANCE EDUCATION: THE VIRTUAL CENTER FOR MODELING

In the preceding chapters, we presented experiences from online distance courses with emphasis on the media and the way they condition interaction and collaboration in virtual learning environments. Based on these experiences, we discussed how knowledge is produced by collectives composed of human and non-human actors, which constitute the basic unit of knowledge production: humans-with-media.

In light of this view of knowledge, in which human and non-human actors are involved in its production, we have been paying special attention to the Internet. Considering how the Internet is becoming available on buses, trains, and even in classrooms, we imagine the day when it will be as common in the classroom as calculators or textbooks, and when its use in the classroom will not be "prohibited". What will be the effects on education? Many of the questions and answers found in textbooks are available on the Internet, or will be soon! If the Internet does in fact become so popular and can be used, little that we consider today to be a problem will survive as such! In this sense, we believe that teaching approaches that prioritize open questions could grow in importance with the presence of the Internet. But what is a problem?

More than two decades ago, Saviani (1985) and Borba (1987) defined a problem as something that has a subjective part, which is related to a personal interest, and an objective part, associated with an obstacle that presents itself in the experience of a person or group. In this context, many of the activities presented in the classroom today would no longer be considered problems, having become commonplace, and their answers would be available on the Internet. Nowadays, if someone wants to know something about a given subject, they have only to access a search site on the Internet, and various answers to standardized problems will be found. For example, if one carries out a search using the word "function", innumerable references to first and second degree functions appear, as well as definitions, examples, and exercises. Thus, in an educational context, it would seem that teaching approaches that value searching, elaboration, and reflection based on what is already known would be most appropriate if the Internet were to be fully admitted into face-to-face or virtual classrooms.

63

In this chapter, drawing on the theoretical issues discussed earlier, we will present a pedagogical focus called Modeling that we believe to be in synergy with Information and Communication Technologies (ICTs), and with the Internet in particular, to the extent that it can generate challenging problems that encourage experimentation and elaboration of problems by the students themselves.

MATHEMATICAL MODELING AND ITS SYNERGY WITH INFORMATION AND COMMUNICATION TECHNOLOGIES

One alternative for incorporating the Internet into the classroom is using mathematical modeling, understood by us as a pedagogical strategy that privileges students' choices of themes to be investigated, thus facilitating their comprehension of how mathematical contents addressed in the classroom relate to everyday issues. Various authors, such as Araújo (2002), Jacobini (2004), Almeida and Dias (2004), and Machado Júnior et al. (2006), among others, have developed experiences using this pedagogical approach.

Modeling, which can be considered similar to project-based pedagogy, has various conceptions that differentiate it, basically depending on the emphasis on the selection of the problem to be investigated. This selection can be made by the teacher, can result from an agreement between the teacher and students, or the students can be allowed to choose a subject that they want to investigate. One of the main characteristics of modeling is dealing with open problems, which can lead to a departure from the structure of the curriculum. Our view of modeling is based on students' choice of themes, so that the teacher acts as the mediator in the investigative process, presenting different paths for transforming the theme into modeling projects.

From this perspective, which privileges investigation and exploration, we believe modeling is in synergy with ICTs. Examples presented by Borba and Penteado (2001), Malheiros (2004), and Borba and Villarreal (2005) illustrate this synergy based on research conducted since 1993 on modeling projects developed by university students in a Biological Sciences program at São Paulo State University (UNESP), Rio Claro campus, Brazil. In these projects, ICTs appear as actors at various levels, for example: word processing programs are used to type the projects; specific software programs are used to sketch tables and graphs, and graphing calculators aid in the exploration and investigation of data previously collected.

In recent years, with the increasing presence of the Internet on the UNESP campus, we noticed that students in this course were using the Internet to conduct bibliographic searches for their modeling projects. For some themes chosen by the students, for example "mad cow disease", in 2001, it would have been difficult to find references in books, periodicals, and journals. Often, as in this case, students choose a theme precisely because of its novelty and its repercussions in society, and in such cases, the Internet is the only alternative for data collection – and consequently, to develop the research – as no books on the subject are available yet in libraries. The Web becomes an enormous digital library which makes it possible to develop certain modeling projects, characterizing the webgraphy of the projects, as highlighted by Borba and Villarreal (2005).

In another instance, the Internet assumed a role that went beyond a primary source for consultations. In a project entitled "The Chloroplasts" in 1999, the students, after having chosen their theme, conducted research using the Internet and other sources and found descriptions of procedures and results of experiments related to their theme. They were able to carry out the experiments in laboratories on campus, and upon checking the results, discovered that they differed from those reported on the Internet. They repeated the experiment, and this time obtained results that approximated those they had found on the Internet. In this case, it was as though the Internet was used as a collaborator or verifier in the interpretation of results of biology experiments.

The Internet has assumed still other roles in the development of modeling projects, including means of communication between students and professor, and among students themselves, mainly by e-mail but also via MSN[1] and Orkut[2] (DINIZ, 2007).

In this sense, we see that the Internet acts differently in different groups of students and can be used in modeling projects as a source of information, collaborator in analysis, or means of communication. For us, this is yet another facet of what Borba and Villarreal (2005) point to as the active role of technology in knowledge production, supporting the thesis that knowledge is produced by collectives of humans-with-media. We believe that, with this, the Internet transforms modeling projects and, consequently, modeling itself, in that it makes the investigation of certain subjects possible, enables communication and discussion of those subjects, and can even collaborate in activities involving experiments.

During the development of modeling projects, the teacher is a participatory agent in the entire process, seeking to guide students as they elaborate activities, regardless of who selects the theme. In this way, one notices that many teachers feel uncomfortable using modeling in the classroom, as challenges may arise that lead them to reformulate their practice in order to achieve their objectives. This process constitutes a transition from the comfort zone into the risk zone, as pointed out by Penteado (2001). It can be a difficult transition for teachers to abandon what is seen as the traditional way of teaching and begin to work with pedagogical approaches in which one cannot always predict the questions that may arise or the best way to deal with them.

Given the difficulties in the school context related to the teaching practice itself or teachers' insecurity with respect to working with modeling, and feeling the need for a virtual locus for collaborative discussion and research on questions related to modeling in online distance education, the first author of this book had the idea to create a virtual environment where such issues could be addressed: the Virtual Center for Modeling (VCM).

Our experiences prior to the VCM led us to reflect on the role of the Internet and the way it transforms modeling in face-to-face education, which is beyond the scope of this book. When we considered them in the context of online distance education, we encountered other possibilities for educating and being educated, over distance with the Internet, and the VCM is one example.

THE VIRTUAL CENTER FOR MODELING

Previously we discussed the synergy between modeling and ICTs, which formed the basis for the conception and creation of the VCM. The center was created to become an environment for exchange and mutual support among professors and professor-researchers who use modeling as a pedagogical focus, as well as undergraduate and graduate students who experience this process in class or are interested in the topic, located in different regions of Brazil and even outside of Brazil. One of the objectives of the VCM is to foment collaboration among professors and others interested in modeling, as well as promote the development of collaborative research.

We believe that the creation of an environment that enables professors and researchers to address questions related to teaching and research on modeling can aid teachers in their educational practice as well as contribute to research on the theme. Thus, collaboration is the main challenge of the VCM, with the proposal to make it a "welcoming" environment that deals with difficulties encountered by teachers as they work with modeling in the classroom.

The VCM was implemented at the end of 2005 using the TIDIA-Ae[3] platform, which possesses various tools for synchronous communication (like chat and instant messaging) as well as asynchronous (like forum portfolio, e-mail, and others). It also has a hypertext tool that functions as a collaborative, asynchronous text editor in which fonts, colors, and sizes can be modified, and tables, figures, and links to sites and files can be inserted. In addition, different areas can be created according to the interests of the users. One tool recently implanted in the environment is support material, where material of any nature can be made available to users.

Currently, the VCM has 250 participants, including undergraduate and graduate students, teachers from the elementary, high school, and university levels, and professor-researchers from various institutions across the country. To access it, a login identification and password are needed[4]. After logging in, users of the Center find various activities and reports related to modeling.

66

As an illustration, we can mention the creation of different forums, some related to academic research, in which references and rich discussions were established based on the collaboration of VCM members. This was the case, for example, of one researcher who, seeking to map theses and dissertations written on modeling in mathematics education, started a forum in the VCM to aid in his investigation. Professor-researchers from various locales in the country helped him by contributing references or indicating where to find them.

The relation between project work and modeling was the focus of another forum, proposed by one of the authors of this book, who was at that time studying the two themes and their possible intersections. VCM collaborators suggested references and offered their opinions, which were of fundamental importance for the study being conducted.

In the context of the classroom, the VCM forum was used by teachers who had doubts about certain issues involving modeling. For example, one group of students had chosen Nietzsche as the theme of their project. The teacher responsible, the first author of this book, had doubts regarding what paths to suggest to the students, who were first year biology students enrolled in an applied mathematics course, to help them relate the theme to mathematics. In search of help, a forum was opened soliciting contributions from colleagues. The collaboration from participants in the VCM was rich, with many pertinent suggestions and questions, like the following:

> Perhaps the following ideas will help the biology students: Nietzsche is a thinker who looks at social reality from a truthful, elemental, realist point of view, like that of NATURE, challenging conventional moral positions (embodied in the ideas of SuperMan, the AntiChrist, etc.). Nietzsche, in "Will to Power", makes reference to Darwin's Theory of Evolution. Some authors believe Nietzsche intended to take Darwin's theory further, when he said "what man wants, …, is a bonus of power" and not the self-conservation of the species. If we consider that the Theory of Evolution is a "model" to look at reality like a mathematical model, why not construct the "model" of reality planted by Nietzsche? (message posted 28/04/2006 by Maria Mina)

> [...] I have thought much on the subject. I have followed everyone's suggestions, and each time, I question myself more. If we are proclaiming a Critical Education in which mathematics is only one and not the only way to understand the world, why so much questioning to force mathematics into the work? I think that, even if it is secondary, your students will have the opportunity to know Nietzsche more deeply. There will be a change in behavior in relation to the subject. Don't you think that suffices? Or do you want mathematics to appear as the principal object? Was I able to make myself understood? (message posted 3/5/2006 by Clarissa Nina)

As we can observe, questions regarding the need for the presence of mathematics in a modeling project, suggestions for possible relations between the theme proposed by the students and mathematical contents, and others, were presented and debated by participants from Brazil and Argentina. In addition to the previous suggestions for the professor who asked for help, one of the participants showed interest in the results of the project, asking about its final version. For this, the professor responsible opened another forum and let people know the summary of the project was available in the VCM, and various participants wrote that, based on what they had read, they had become motivated to study and learn more about the philosopher.

> Hello Professor Marcelo!
>
> Nietzsche has enchanted me...
>
> Since the controversy arose, I have been thinking about the subject constantly. Last week I went to a library ... and took out a book on him: "Thus Spoke Zarathustra". I plan to understand a little about this man to be able to offer my opinion. (message posted in the forum on 16/8/2006 by Clarissa Nina).
>
> [...] Yes, I confess that I, too, took off on this one: library inside and "Thus Spoke Zarathustra" under my arm, it seems this shared experience enchanted our minds... It sparked our curiosity about conceptions involving the Being and the Universe... And what does this have to do with mathematics??? And Nietzsche got: 44 messages on the form, virtual and real discussions, book searches, research, analyses, reflections... And the motive? The Calculus in Biology course... One group of students who remained true to their ideology... a professor who sought to share his distress with other professors... The virtual world indicates so many paths, but does not determine precepts for the way we walk... (message posted on 17/8/2006 by Adriana Magedanza).

As the one responsible for instigating the arousing exchange, Marcelo C. Borba invited the group to reflect on the possibilities for seeking support in the environment, and the incitement it can provide its members. His message also illustrated how some questions about themes such as philosophy and philosophy of education permeate the discussion. In addition to this situation-problem faced by the creator of the VCM in his own classroom, other colleagues also presented themes that aroused discussion, such as ethnomathematics in the school, mathematical modeling and mathematical finance. In both cases, suggestions were presented by the proponents of the respective themes, which provoked interesting and elucidating discussions.

Discussions of a theoretical nature were also proposed by participants in the VCM, as well as the dissemination of a project entitled Mathematical Modeling and Presidential Elections, led by Otávio Jacobini. The researchers' idea was to collect information regarding voting intentions near voting locations during the Brazilian Presidential elections in 2006 to afterwards explore statistical techniques related to tables, graphs, and percentages. Upon being disseminated, some VCM participants expressed interest in participating in the project, illustrating once again that the objective of encouraging collaboration was being achieved. Some teachers applied a questionnaire provided by the researchers to their own students, and with their guidance, then tabulated the information, sharing it by e-mail or through the VCM, and disseminating the final results of the research.

In addition to the forums proposed by the users of the VCM, other activities were carried out, including thematic chat sessions. Proposals for themes were provided by participants themselves using the VCM and its resources. Online meetings were scheduled to discuss such themes as Modeling and Teacher Education, Modeling and the Environment, Modeling and Learning Cycles, and Modeling and Ethnomathematics. In all of these sessions, specialists on the theme were invited to participate in the discussions. There was also a session in which the VCM was presented to participants and another in which questions regarding the Fifth National Conference on Modeling and Mathematics Education were discussed, prior to it taking place. All the records of these chat sessions were made available to VCM users so that even those who were unable to follow the discussions for some reason would have access to what was discussed.

Publications on modeling can also be found in the VCM. Theses, dissertations, articles, annals of events related to the theme and out-of-print books can be accessed by participants in the VCM. The VCM provides, in this way, a space to disseminate publications, as all interested users can annex their publications, as well as the beginning of a digital library on Mathematical Modeling.

The VCM also provides the opportunity to disseminate projects that have been developed or are in progress in different contexts. Using the hypertext tool, for example, one can find references to a project being developed entitled "The Mathematical Trail in Ouro Preto", as well as the link to their site[5] for additional information. Descriptions of teaching experiences of the first author of this book in the Biology course are also available in the VCM. One project carried out in Córdoba, Argentina, with children aged 10 and 11, is illustrated with related publications on the theme. Critical Mathematics Education and Modeling is another subject addressed in the VCM.

The community that constitutes the Center uses it in accordance with their objectives and practices, composing a collaborative environment for the investigation, discussion, and dissemination of questions related to modeling in mathematics education. As we have illustrated, various forms of collaboration take place, but not all of them flow smoothly within this virtual community. For example, there are immense technical issues that sometimes abort fruitful discussions.

Toward the end of 2006, participants were enthusiastically engaged in a chat led by professors Adilson Espírito Santo and Tânia Lobato, both of the

State University of Pará[6], when the server for the TIDIA-Ae platform suddenly locked up. It is likely that those of you who have participated in online activities have had similar experiences, and are therefore aware of the difficulties of recovering the same level of enthusiasm after the connection has been reestablished. In this case, we attempted to pick up the discussion where we had left off using the forum tool, but participation was low until it was deactivated.

There are some members of the modeling community whose participation in congresses and other forums is noteworthy, but who have not yet been able to lead activities in the Center, even when invited and offered the full technical support that the VCM can provide through financed projects that make available a network of technicians and students who support it. A study is currently being developed to investigate the reason for this modest participation.

We would like to emphasize that the VCM has made participation and collaboration possible, but it has also faced problems. Borba and Malheiros (2007) analyzed the problems encountered, up to the time of the study, in the way the environment was conceived. Thus, we developed research in the VCM as we studied its problems and the different forms of participation we identified up until that time. We are aware that other studies are underway, but we do not know how they are being undertaken and will only learn about them when they are published in periodicals or in the VCM. Following, however, we present partial results of a study developed in the Center using modeling and online distance education in a different manner from that which led to the conception of the VCM.

DEVELOPING MODELING PROJECTS IN DISTANCE EDUCATION

As described above, various activities are developed in the VCM, and in 2006, the Trends in Mathematics Education course, described in Chapter II, was one of them. This version of the course, however, differed in that the mathematics education trends studied were related to modeling, for example, Teacher Education and Modeling. For this reason, the course was entitled "Trends in Mathematics Education: emphasis on mathematical modeling". It was proffered by two of the authors of this book who, in the process of planning it, imagined the possibility of participants developing modeling projects via distance. Behind this proposal was the conception that, in addition to theoretical studies on this pedagogical strategy, it would be important for the teachers, while students, to develop modeling projects to become familiar with the process.

The dynamic of the course was basically the same as previous versions except that the teacher-students, in pairs, chose themes and elaborated modeling projects. The projects were developed during extra hours outside the chat sessions, some of which were dedicated to discussing them. The two final classes were specifically dedicated to presentation and discussion of the projects developed by the pairs of teacher-students. To elaborate the projects, an area was opened in the virtual learning environment for each of the pairs to which only they and the professors had access. One of the professors, who was conducting research on the theme[7], was primarily responsible for advising the students on their projects. Other course participants were exposed to other students' projects only during the discussions that arose during the synchronous sessions. Versions were also made available to everyone in a common area prior to the classes dedicated to presentation of the projects.

In our experience with this course, we observed various ways that mathematics teacher-students, who in most cases, had never met face-to-face, developed modeling projects entirely via distance,

First, the choice of the theme deserves to be highlighted. For teachers who had already worked with modeling or studied it as a pedagogical approach, the choice of the subject to be investigated emerged very naturally based on their own interests regarding a given subject. This was the case, for example, of the pair of teachers named Clarissa and Silvana, who investigated telephone landlines in the state of Rio Grande do Sul. For Silvana, it was important to discover which was the best plan in that state, as she was planning to change telephone companies. Another pair composed of teachers from Argentina modeled a problem that had been presented to them by their students. It was a transportation problem that involved determining the "best" timing for a stoplight so they could arrive as rapidly as possibly at school.

Meanwhile, most of the teachers who had never worked with or studied modeling as a pedagogical approach were concerned about what grade level a given theme could be worked on. The simple act of choosing a subject and investigating it, and later modeling it, was difficult, as it was not possible to determine a priori the mathematical contents that should possibly be used for that theme. Nevertheless, the teacher-students appeared to choose themes from their everyday lives without worrying about the level of mathematics that could appear in the projects, especially after some theoretical discussions and conversations with the professors of the course.

Another aspect that we feel is important to highlight is related to the role of ICTs in the development of the modeling projects. The TIDIA-Ae environment has various tools that were used in different ways by the pairs of students. For all of them, the decision regarding the topic to be explored occurred in online conversations that took place via various means, including e-mail, MSN, and the chat tool. Some developed practically their entire project using resources available in the TIDIA-Ae environment, while others used it only to post versions of their projects for the professors to access.

In addition to the environment, other resources were used for communication, such as MSN, the telephone (in two isolated cases), as well as e-mail. This information was obtained in interviews conducted with the teacher-students individually after the course had ended, via chat in the virtual learning environment.

The ICTs were fundamental actors in the development of the projects, as they were present in all of them, albeit in different ways. Each pair organized themselves as they felt most comfortable to communicate with their partner and with the professors. This was due, among other things, to the freedom given to the participants by the professors, who did not require that communication be done only by e-mail or within the environment, for example. Although it was hoped that the teacher-students would mainly use the hypertext tool to elaborate their modeling projects, because of its capabilities for collaborative edition of texts, this was not required, and the participants followed different paths to develop their modeling projects. In order for the reader to better understand how this development occurred, we will briefly present the paths and steps taken by the teacher-students in one of the projects.

The pair composed of the teacher-students Clarissa and Silvana, who developed the project on telephone landlines, began collecting data from the websites of the telephone companies they planned to research. Based on the information they found, they presented a question to the professors of the course regarding charges for random pulses by one of the companies, using the hypertext tool.

> The service is measured by pulses. Each pulse (with taxes included) costs R$ 0.16314. And they explain that, on weekdays between 6am and 12am, and Saturdays from 6am to 2pm, one pulse is charged for completing the call plus one pulse every 4 minutes. On other days and periods, they charge only one pulse per call. HOWEVER, another time, on the same site that provided the data about the pulses, cost, and time periods, they presented a table with the prices per minute (with pulses included), varying according to the time of the call. [...] I found this information confusing and conflicting. Do they measure pulses and charge per pulse or per minute? [...]
>
> So I decided to go to the Anatel site to clarify things. There I discovered that Anatel asks the phone companies to present the cost of the calls in minutes. (But isn't it strange that the system of measurement is pulse while the charges are presented minutes?)

Based on these questions, the pair discussed the problem further and their next steps for the project using the chat tool. One of them mentioned she had made a graph to sketch the charges made by pulse:

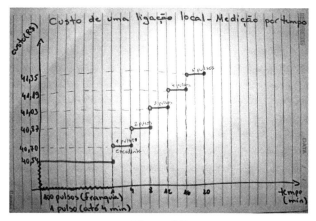

Figure 17

Since Clarissa did not have a scanner, she took a digital photograph of the graph (FIG. 17) and posted it in the environment so we could visualize it. Here was see the digital camera participating in the process of visualization of the behavior of charges made per pulse, constituting a thinking collective of humans-with-digital-camera-and-Internet. After discussing how to compare the data of the telephone companies analyzed, since they were of a different nature, Clarissa and Silvana decided, based on the suggestion of one of the professors, to create generic situations and explore them. In addition, they compared the plans offered by the companies, analyzing their advantages and disadvantages individually.

To develop their project, in addition to using the TIDIA-Ae environment to present their questions, the pair used MSN to communicate between themselves and with the professors. The files containing versions of the projects were typed using Word, and the graphs were plotted using Excel.

The professor provided some comments, criticisms, and suggestions to the students based on the first version of their project, which they incorporated into the next version to the extent possible. This exchange took place several times, and this feedback procedure was similar to that used to communicate between themselves: the Word file was read, saved with another name after inserting comments and questions in the body of the text, which were highlighted with another color (chosen and informed at the beginning of the text in the same file). The final version of the project was presented to the group in the second-to-last synchronous meeting, after having been posted beforehand in hypertext for the other participants to read and discuss.

With the Internet as the means of communication that permeated the entire course, data gathering for the modeling projects was no different, with all but two pairs using the web to collect data. The teacher-students also presented their projects virtually to the other participants, and during and after their presentations, the others offered questions and suggestions, thus constituting a virtual collaboration. For this presentation, the teacher-students had prior access to the projects in order to be able to interact and collaborate with their colleagues. In this sense, a collective of human and non-human actors was formed for the purpose of understanding various issues, such as the recording industry and CD piracy, recycling and composting of waste, as well as other themes, permeated by modeling as a pedagogical strategy.

The practice of developing modeling projects, throughout the Trends course, was for most teacher-students, the first time they were "doing" modeling as students, although some of them had already used modeling as a pedagogical strategy in their classrooms. Participants reported that the elaboration of the projects via distance led to a different understanding of modeling, and this was made possible thanks to the Internet, among other things, as well as the virtual environment being used, TIDIA-Ae.

The application of the projects in the classroom by participants was not our objective, but this is what happened in the case of two of the projects. The teacher-students, who were doing modeling for the first time, felt that the activities they were developing could be taken to their respective classrooms, which is what they did. In one of the cases, part of the project was adapted, and the students also modeled soccer fields. In the other, the students gathered data to evaluate questions related to food and nutrition. The teacher-students reported, in their interviews after the course had ended, that the experience was very interesting, and that they planned to continue using this pedagogical strategy in the classroom. In this sense, the possibility of developing projects via distance enabled the teachers to take the modeling practices into their classrooms.

With the elaboration of the modeling projects in this course, we conjecture that, in addition to the Internet transforming modeling, as discussed earlier, it also transformed the Trends course to the degree that open problems, proposed by the participants, were investigated. In addition, participants put into practice theoretical aspects that they studied in the process of developing their projects, that arose based on their choice of theme.

RESEARCH METHODOLOGY IN ONLINE DISTANCE EDUCATION

In the preceding section, we discussed the development of modeling projects via distance. Throughout this process, a study was being conducted by the second author of this book to investigate how the elaboration of modeling projects takes place via distance. Based on the assumption that the objective of this study is to understand the process of production of projects, the research was of a qualitative nature. At this point, the reader may be asking: But what is doing research online? What does it mean to take qualitative research procedures to virtual environments? Questions like this, and others presented by Borba (2004; 2006), constitute a vast terrain for investigation. One of the new frontiers that members of GPIMEM have explored revolves around research methodology.

In our research group, various studies were conducted in the context of online distance education using qualitative research methodology, based on Lincoln and Guba (1985), Goldenberg (1999), Alves-Mazzotti (2001), and various contributors to the handbook organized by Denzin and Lincoln (2000). These authors and the members of our group defend, in different ways, the importance of the researcher being involved in the context being researched, as opposed to the usual aseptic approaches to investigation in which the researcher strives to maintain as much distance as possible from the object of study. We are aware that, even in the context of distance education, our presence as professors and researchers interferes, conditions, and influences the environment being studied, but it is not yet clear to us whether or not there are differences in this type of influence compared to the usual classroom.

Borba (2004), on the other hand, presented a series of questions about the natural environment in the scenario of education, emphasizing the qualitative approach of Lincoln and Guba (1985), when this occurs in virtual learning environments (VLEs). What would a natural environment be in online distance education? Would a VLE be considered a natural environment? Borba, in this essay, expands on the question. According to him, in chat, the language is "naturally" transcribed, and "the nature [of the] text produced is differentiated; it is a mixture of speech and writing" (p. 309). He emphasizes that this fact is not taken into consideration in research on online distance education of a qualitative nature. The environment of the research is virtual, but he questions whether or not the "different [physical spaces] from where people access the site or chat room" should be investigated, as well. In this article, he presents questions like "What does it mean to conduct an 'interview' via e-mail or chat? How to do the triangulation proposed by Lincoln and Guba (1985) almost 20 years ago as a way to distance our affirmations further from mere opinion" (2004, p.310)

As presented in the previous chapter, the humans-with-media collective is the basic unit that produces knowledge, and media therefore condition this production. But is it possible that they also condition research methodology, seen in the classic sense as the path to knowledge? We believe there are influences, although they cannot be noticed in all dimensions of research methodology. We see methodology as the amalgam of a view of knowledge and the research procedures developed in a given study. We will analyze how some elements of research methodology online are, or are not, being changed, drawing on our experiences with this new educational mode, online distance education.

The Research Question

Defining the research question is one of the main elements of investigation. The research question that guided the study partially presented above took shape as the investigation unfolded, according to the description of Araújo and Borba (2004), characterizing the emergent design of research. In other words, changes in methodological procedures, and even in the focus of the study, may occur during the development of a study, and are important for it, as these changes "indicate movement toward a sophisticated level of investigation that provides greater insight" (LINCOLN; GUBA, 1985, p.229).

But we needed to adopt what Bicudo (1993) calls, according to phenomenology, placing the object in suspension, looking at it without preconceptions, so that it can be seen as it shows itself to our attentive eye, without theoretical lenses. Taking what is seen as aspects of perspectives of that which is under focus, in this case, the elaboration of modeling projects via distance, using analysis and reflection, we sought the meaning of this in light of our question, aiming at its characteristics. This is a process that can point to new aspects (in relation to those commonly affirmed, whether in theories, research, or everyday speech) and warn us against being influenced by previous affirmations, and also against remaining only at the level of the initial manifestations.

While developing research online, we were unable to note significant influences of the Internet on the generation of the research question, except for one rather trivial one: in addition to the discussion with the research group, the Internet made it possible to contact some researchers through the network to discuss the originality and relevance of the question chosen. There is, however, another aspect that we are still studying related to changes in the question of the study described here. We have already seen that it is natural for the question to be modified, in this view of knowledge based on emergent research design. In the study in question, the fact that other Internet interfaces outside the TIDIA-Ae environment were used by course participants led to changes in the research question to account for these forms of communication that were not foreseen by the researcher. This type of change in the question, caused by the way some teacher-students used the Internet, does not seem significant enough to conclude that the Internet shaped the question in the same way it shaped and transformed data collection, but we believe it is important to call readers' attention to deeper analyses on the theme, that we ourselves are currently engaged in, aiming to identify more relevant roles for VLEs in the elaboration of research questions related to online distance education practices.

Data Collection

As presented, the context of the study was the 2006 version of the Trends course, and data collection began when the course began, when the teacher-students began deciding, via chat sessions, who they would work with, and questions regarding the choice of themes for the projects began to emerge. It is worth noting that, with the exception of two pairs, the others had never met face-to-face, and that the production of the projects, in all cases, took place via distance. There were no face-to-face meetings.

After settling on a theme, the pairs began to Interact with the researcher using some tools in the virtual learning environment, as well as e-mail and MSN. All communication between the researcher and the teacher-students during the course, i.e. conversations via chat or MSN, e-mail, as well as material and messages posted in the TIDIA-Ae environment, was automatically recorded. Versions of modeling projects sent beforehand for the researcher's suggestions and criticisms, as well as the final versions, were saved. In addition, individual interviews were conducted with all the participants via chat sessions to clarify some questions regarding the development of their projects, such as the tools they used, their choice of the theme, among others. All of this information composed the body of data for this study. The reader, at this point, may be asking: How was this data collected and organized?

The TIDIA-Ae environment records all data inserted into it and allows them to be recovered, providing a record of tools such as chat and hypertext. The latter, being an asynchronous text editor, allows the recovery of the versions generated and informs who made the last change and when. For example, with each new change or insertion of characters, a new version is created, and when a document is "finished", it may have a large number of versions. In addition, it is possible to recover all of them, and to know the author of each alteration and the date it occurred. The other tools in the environment only store information. During the course, as the participants interacted with each other or with the professor, the data were inserted into the environment, and the researcher converted them into text files and saved them, organizing them according to the student pairs and the tools used.

The interactions that took place between the teacher-students and the researcher by e-mail or MSN were also filed. However, the interactions that took place among participants using these media are not included in the body of data collected for the study. Thus, some information was incomplete, leaving some gaps, as in a puzzle. For this reason, individual interviews were conducted with each participant in order to recover some of the missing "pieces".

The TIDIA-Ae environment was the main actor in the Trends course taught in 2006, participating, from a methodological point of view, in a unique way. It should be noted that data transcription is not necessary in research developed in environments like TIDIA-Ae. Various studies conducted by our group were carried out based on face-to-face situations that were videotaped. In these cases, it was necessary to transcribe the tapes to analyze them. In other cases, interviews were conducted using non-digital audio resources, and transcription was also necessary. The debate regarding the need for complete transcription of the data (BICUDO, 2000; VILLARREAL, 1999; PENTEADO; BORBA, 2000) becomes meaningless in online environments like these, as the transcription is done automatically, which contributes to the trustworthiness of the data. Questions like these lead us to think that the Internet transforms the "doing" of research and some specifics of the methodology used. Note that we not speaking of a black-and-white discussion, since it is possible, as some authors argue, that the act of transcribing is fundamental, although we believe that everyone recognizes it makes no sense for the researcher to transcribe what the platform already transcribes automatically.

The researcher needs to be attentive to the fact that participants in a study based on face-to-face interactions can communicate among themselves in a way similar to online interactions, about research themes without the researcher's knowledge. The online environment naturally facilitates this, at least via e-mail (one-on-one). If we are in a classroom, we can observe the looks exchanged between students or their lack of interest. In a chat or videoconference, we can note silence, but we have no idea what is being said via instant messaging or e-mail. The researcher should use caution when coming to conclusions in a given study, since their data probably represent a more refined cross-section of the interactions among participants than imagined.

Certainly, online research generates immense quantities of data. If on the one hand, it is facilitated by automatic transcription, on the other hand, the researcher will have to get used to online data analysis and the search for procedures for inductively identifying what we have called themes or episodes that allow analysis and presentation of data, as we will discuss below.

Many researchers often get lost trying to identify their research as a "case study", "action research", or "participant observation", among others. In general, we have proposed that the methodology be described and not labeled. This advice appears even more appropriate when we look closely at certain elements of the methodology. For example, the data collected in an online learning environment generates electronic documents, and we could therefore say that one possible line of analysis would be "document analysis". Some may defend that they are documents, as they can be printed, however we would argue that material generated in chat sessions is a mixture of third-order orality with second-order writing. Lévy (1993) wrote that, after writing, a second-order orality emerged that resulted from reading, in contrast to first-order orality that was not linked to reading. Borba and Villarreal (2005) maintain that some of the language developed with the Internet presents characteristics of written speech or spoken writing, from which the idea emerged to call it third-order orality or second-order writing.

Notwithstanding, it is important to avoid getting caught up with names and understand that the plasticity of ICTs leaves at least some doubt with respect to whether records of chat sessions can be considered "documents", an expression normally associated with more durable objects.

Thus, it would be best to avoid labeling your data as documents or not and instead say if they originated from forum, a chat session, hypertext, or some other tool, thus allowing the reader familiar with these computer interfaces to understand if the interactions were predominantly multilogue, quasi-sequential linear debate, or collaborative writing, characteristics associated, respectively, with the tools above. In addition, however, the researcher should also describe, in general terms, what the interation was like in this chat, for example.

Data Analysis

In the preceding discussion, the reader may have wondered if we were referring to data collection or data analysis. Martins and Bicudo (2005) argue that qualitative research methodology should be of a theoretical and a practical nature, i.e., the work of data collection and analysis should be related, at all times, with the theoretical interrogations being pursued and studied by the researcher, points we reiterate, as we believe analysis begins together with the data collection. Thus, the researcher should have the research question in mind and look at the data, as it is being collected, seeking to identify possible "answers". An example of this was the decision to conduct interviews at the end of the course. The need for the interviews was perceived because the researcher was closely studying the data, and interacting with it, throughout the process of information gathering.

During the process of data collection, the researcher began early on to organize the data. In this phase, the researcher is also doing analysis as she "classifies" her data according to certain "criteria". In this example, the data was organized according to pairs of students. The information referring to each pair was organized chronologically, as the objective of the study was to understand how the elaboration of modeling projects occurs via distance. All the data, from the choice of theme to the interviews, was then catalogued and printed to "begin" analysis. On the other hand, the digitalized data made it possible to use the search tools to locate key words associated with a given classification.

The analysis process itself is long and solitary, as the researcher interacts with her data in search of clues regarding the research question. As we have emphasized, this process begins for us during data collection and acquires form as the researcher visualizes what she plans to present. In the case of the study highlighted here, the first big challenge was to present the data to the reader. What to present, and how to present it? The volume of data generated was considerable, exceeding 1,500 pages. How to transform this information into a few pages that explained "everything" considered relevant to the research?

Araújo and Borba (2004), among others, believe that the use of different procedures can influence study results, and therefore emphasize triangulation as a possible way to increase the credibility of research developed using a qualitative approach.

Denzin and Lincoln (2000) affirm that triangulation is not a tool or strategy for validation, but rather an alternative to increase validation, and add that the combination of various methodological procedures contributes better understanding and analysis of the data, with the purpose of broadening the description, explanation, and comprehension of the phenomenon studied. According to Lincoln and Guba (1985), triangulation of methods is one technique to improve the interpretation of data, leading to greater credibility at the moment it is analyzed.

In the study we presented, triangulation occurred to the extent that various methodological procedures were used to analyze the data. As we have already suggested, the nature of the writing in a chat is qualitatively different from a message posted in the forum, for example, because of the very nature of the communication established in these different tools, one being synchronous and in real time, and the other asynchronous. In this way, triangulation can aid in the interpretation of data, conferring greater reliability. In our example, the researcher opted to describe some moments she considered relevant for the elaboration of the modeling projects via distance, chronologically, such as the process of choosing a theme, the media used to develop the projects, the presentation of the projects to the others during the synchronous meeting via chat, etc. For each of these moments, a description was elaborated with excerpts from chat sessions or other tools with the aim of increasing trustworthiness. Some of the expressions used, graphs drawn – any information considered relevant – were "transcribed" exactly as their authors executed them.

After the data were presented, together with the theoretical reference adopted for the study, the final stage of analysis was carried out, always keeping in mind the research question. At this moment, then, the researcher shows evidence for the results obtained, comparing them with the theory on which the study was based.

Another procedure recommended by authors like Lincoln and Guba (1985) for more than two decades is followed by GPIMEM when, in our weekly meetings, we discuss the analyses of group members' projects that are in progress. This procedure, called "peer review", aids in the analysis to the degree that the researchers must defend their interpretations and refute alternative interpretations. This procedure has been expanded, as research group members who live in other cities, or are unable to attend the meeting for some reason, can participate asynchronously, via e-mail, or synchronously in meetings and defenses. On such occasions, we have used Skype[8] and MSN as tools. In this way, the Internet has allowed the extension of this part of the research methodology, at the same time it enables the group to maintain its virtual ties.

The Literature Review

As we commented at the beginning of this chapter, the Internet has been used by students to develop modeling projects in face-to-face teaching situations. When projects are developed on the web, is in the Trends course described here, the Internet becomes a "natural" source of research. Internet-based search engines are used often for various types of research in the educational context. And how does this occur with academic research?

The literature review for a study is composed of a set of publications that are in consonance with the research problem, and in this sense, they should inform the study, making it possible to map investigations and results related to a given theme. We believe there are no models to be followed, but rather that common sense is the most useful strategy for composing a literature review, together with the research methodology, which consists of the methodological procedures, which should be consonant with the view of knowledge. And this is also true for sources on the Internet. We often locate texts to download from Internet sites of recognized academic institutions and include them in our literature reviews. Well-known periodicals make their articles available on the web, some paid and others for free. These are some examples of sources that are considered "reliable" in the academic environment, illustrating how the virtual nature of the World Wide Web of computers is impregnated with social aspects. Diniz (2007) observed, in his research, that undergraduate students in a face-to-face classroom, engaged in projects to model themes of their own choosing, also used criteria impregnated with social aspects to decide whether or not a site was reliable.

However, there are many websites of questionable reliability, such as Wikipedia, a virtual encyclopedia based on Wiki Pages, which are so-called "open" web pages which allow many people to alter and include contents. When we entered the Portuguese Wikipedia, we found the phrase "the free encyclopedia that everyone can edit". This would be one possible definition for this encyclopedia, and the fact anyone can alter its contents renders it "suspect" by academia. We have also had the experience of "citing" something from Wikipedia, and when someone went to "check" it, the content was completely different. We are not arguing against using Wikipedia as a source of information, although there is an ongoing debate regarding its use in academic work and false information inserted into it. It is therefore important to verify the information found in Wikipedia in other sources.

Conducting a review of the literature involves mapping the existing work on the subject under study, and nowadays, the Internet is commonly used to aid in the search for material with characteristics that converge with the investigation being carried out. The web is a vast library, and it would be difficult to not find what we seek, but common sense should predominate to guarantee that only reliable data is used.

THE "NATURAL" ENVIRONMENT OF THE INTERNET

For many, the Internet can be understood as virtual in the sense of being the opposite of real. Some even understand it as an escape, since the word "virtual" is often used to designate something that is not real, "whereas 'reality' assumes a material effectiveness, a tangible presence" (LÉVY, 1999, p.47). This author emphasizes that virtual is not opposed to real, but rather to the current, and says that "the virtual is real" (p.48), i.e., that it exists without being present; the virtual does not substitute the real, or the natural, but rather widens opportunities to develop experiences in different contexts, like classrooms or teaching experiments, and these can generate research. Lévy (1993) also calls attention to the "new ways of thinking and being-together [that] are being elaborated in the world of telecommunications and informatics" (p.7), and highlights that "relations between men, work, and intelligence itself depends, in fact, on the incessant metamorphosis of informational devices of all kinds" (p.7).

We hope we have convinced the reader that relations on the web are impregnated with connections among researchers, the researched, collaborators, etc. In other words, social relations become established and, more clearly in some cases than in others, transform the way we do research, for example. This is what we refer to as "the role of the Internet", which acts to shape speech and help create languages that increasingly combine written text, orality of various orders, images, sound, and animation.

These changes brought by the web may be unsettling to those who were not familiar with it before, or still are not, and at the same time, they help to define what it means to be human at the beginning of the 21st Century. Even the lives of those who have no access to the Internet have nevertheless begun to be shaped by it, in the same way the lives of the landless and homeless are shaped by the concentration of private property in the hands of a few.

For Lincoln and Guba (1985), conducting research in a natural context suggests that the actors of the study cannot be understood in isolation from the context; in addition, they argue that in the act of observation, for example, the researcher becomes influenced by what is seen, and thus, the interaction between research and researcher should be constant to improve comprehension of the phenomenon being studied. In this sense, the question posed by Borba (2004) appears to have been answered: the virtual environment can be considered natural, according to the meaning intended by Lincoln and Guba (1985) as being in contrast to controlled research environments. The Internet already impregnates our lives, as it does parks, schools, and other "natural" environments where researchers strive to connect their understandings with people's lived experiences. The web is natural; it has already changed humans, and collectives of humans-with-Internet are already protagonists in educational contexts, shaping ways of thinking and producing knowledge, no longer perceived as "E.T.'s". Already students are arriving to study in schools and universities without any "accent" in relation to using the Internet. At the beginning of the 21st Century, it already permeates the human condition.

Based on accounts of experiences in the VCM, we believe the Internet can enable new practices in education, and particularly in mathematics education, through the constitution of new communities that become involved around a theme to debate, collaborate, and learn about issues in the context of academia as well as schools. In addition, we inferred that the practices presented, such as the development of modeling projects, are examples of activities developed in the context of online distance education that are transformed by the scenario in which they are carried out.

CHAPTER VI

TEACHING PRACTICE AND OTHER DIMENSIONS IN ONLINE DISTANCE EDUCATION

In this book, we have addressed various aspects of online distance education. We have tried to present details regarding how it takes place, how it materializes using chat rooms, videoconferences, or other interfaces. We saw how the notion of humans-with-media can support a view of online distance education that emphasizes the type of interaction we have with the different interfaces used in learning environments. Our intention was to allow the reader to analyze what can occur in this educational modality and, in this way, avoid a dualistic debate about online distance education.

In doing so, we defend a model for online courses that is based on small classes to increase the possibility of intense interaction with participants. In particular, we show how this model can have an impact in face-to-face classrooms, as it allows teachers to simultaneously participate in an online course and receive the support they need as they introduce innovations into their teaching practice. Such a model is opposed to virtual practices that involve merely "downloading files" and rapid online evaluations of students.

Above all, it is necessary to adopt a critical attitude. We are aware that it is not very common to have the opportunity to conduct online courses like the ones we have presented here, with limited numbers of participants and more than one professor. Similarly, we also know that teaching experiences, especially in mathematics, that can be based on videoconference technology and have specialized technical support – and that are so close to future teachers - are rare. Having access is one step, and appropriate technologies are also key, but most important is the pedagogical work associated with the use of the Internet.

We also addressed online practices that are not based on the notion of a course, as in the case of the Virtual Center for Modeling, which can be seen as a virtual community under construction that discusses an important trend in mathematics education: modeling. As described above, we understand modeling as a pedagogical approach in which students actively participate in decision making regarding problems to be studied in the classroom. Research projects have been developed and experiences have been shared on this website - practices which can be considered "professional self-development" - in which the teachers involved initiate forums, chat sessions, and other forms of interaction, according to the sub-theme related to the modeling activity.

There are other extremely relevant themes that we have only touched on, however, such as public policies regarding online distance education, or even how distance education concentrates professional education in a few regions of the country. This choice was purposeful, as we have consolidated research on the themes we opted to present and only initial reflections regarding the others.

We also touched only briefly on the rich experience of participating in the TIDIA-Ae Project, which provided the opportunity for our research group, GPIMEM, to participate with other groups, mostly from the field of Computer Sciences, in the construction of a virtual learning environment. This chance for a group like ours, from the field of education, to generate demands for the development of the platform, and in the process, understand the limits of those demands and hear the suggestions of other groups, contributed significantly to help our group mature. Experiencing interdisciplinarity, currently very much in vogue but not always practiced, was an important part of our experience as participants in the creation of – and not only users of - a platform to support online distance education.

We have not referred to studies on electronic games via the Internet, like those of Rosa and Maltempi (2006), or the issue of online evaluation being developed by Kenski and colleagues of Educacional[1]. Nor did we address other important topics of the virtual world, like electronic mailing lists. The e-mail list of the Brazilian Society of Mathematics Education (*Sociedade Brasileira de Educação Matemática*, SBEM)[2], for example, has been an important medium in which everyone-talks-to-everyone, ideas are generated for articles, and heated debates take place not only about mathematics education, but about all kinds of related subjects. The list is characterized by a conception that our specific field of interest is interrelated with practically every other dimension of knowledge. Furthermore, this list has become a virtual locus in which people speak in a personal tone, conversing about soccer or other themes as they might in a bar or café.

Another project currently underway that we will only mention briefly is the Digital Mathematical Performance Project[3], aimed at studying the possibilities for synergy between mathematics education and theories originating from the arts, when these take place in the virtual world. This international collaboration, involving researchers from Canada and Brazil, is a live example of how the Internet enables communities to form based on the interests of those involved, regardless of geographic location. The project is structured in such a way that samples of the theoretical articles, or even digital mathematical artifacts that are created, are made available on the website to anyone who is interested in the project.

However, one theme that has already been addressed throughout this book and deserves to be discussed in greater depth is the issue of the online teacher. As we observed, online distance education has various dimensions, some of which we have discussed in this book. Even if we look only at the aspect of teaching, it is multifaceted. We already discussed some specifics of teaching, such as the development of new strategies by the teacher according to the interfaces used. In chat, the teacher will need to type rapidly if he wants to participate in the discussion of themes in a multilogue, in which participants choose different and simultaneous paths to interact in the synchronous debate. In the case of videoconference, the teacher must know how to speak slowly and manage the environment at the same time she is speaking. In both cases, the preparation and attempt to coax the "virtual shy people" to participate is a challenge that requires special attention.

Through the lens of mathematics education, we cannot fail to mention here the relation between the learning environment created during the course and the education of the teachers involved. The way a teacher learns this process can condition the way they perceive and develop mathematics in their own classroom. It enables reflection on important elements of the learning process, such as conjecturing about specific problems, exchanging ideas, elaborating justifications, and others. The courses were planned based on conceptions of distance mathematics education in which dialoguing, discussing mathematical concepts, making mistakes, interacting, collaborating, etc., are considered relevant to "doing" mathematics. As they discussed mathematics, the teacher-students stated their positions regarding how to work in the classroom with the mathematical content being studied. In our online courses, we sought to value the professors' knowledge and the teachers' knowledge, as well, and we believe this book illustrates that an online environment can meet the recommendations of researchers in the field of teacher education. In other words, it is possible to work collaboratively, reflect on practice, and share experiences.

We also observed that, because we prioritized personalized interaction, our course model demands considerable asynchronous participation, as well. Sending e-mails to participants with suggestions for possible paths to solve mathematical problems, or to address a given topic they read about, demands time and the ability to deal with someone you cannot see. Unlike face-to-face relations, in which gestures, tone of voice, and corrections can resolve a misunderstanding, in the asynchronous relation, via email, this becomes more difficult.

In our research experiences, we always had two professors, one who dealt with the synchronous part of the course and the other with the asynchronous part. In some models of courses, the work of following the asynchronous interactions has assumed a secondary role. To emphasize this, expressions like tutor or animator have been used to refer to this professional. The title of teacher is often reserved only for a few people who give lectures and may have little or no interaction with the virtual participants in a course or similar activity.

If we have criticized, from a pedagogical perspective, models that fail to emphasize interaction, the criticism of these distinctions between tutor and teacher should be taken even further. This does not mean to say that, if the term tutor is used, the role of the teacher is automatically being diminished. But at this moment, when the creation of a special Federal government fund is being discussed to guarantee better salaries for education professionals in Brazil, and small progress is being made in the form of a minimum salary for teachers, it would be very dangerous not to call this professional a teacher. Such considerations regarding labor rights may apply in other countries, as well.

We understand that a radical improvement in teachers' salaries is the fundamental issue for teachers to be more respected by different groups – students, parents, government, and society in general – and to increase the number of people who choose teaching as a profession not as something temporary, but as a life project, as often it is abandoned due to low salaries. It is fundamental, therefore, that despite the specificities of the online teacher, the title of teacher be attributed to those who in fact exercise that role. The person who responds to e-mails or is present in the face-to-face classroom helping a student cope with a given problem is a teacher and should be designated as such.

We cannot allow online distance education to create a class of professionals with no rights, in the same way some are attempting to end authorship of online material as a strategy to avoid paying already underpaid, and sometimes unpaid, copyrights. We know this practice is also affecting those who develop course books for face-to-face courses, but it is gaining ground in the emerging online courses. Material available on the Internet may be free, but without a doubt, the author of material developed for a course should be paid just as the teacher is paid. In the case of free, public courses, one cannot expect these professionals to adopt an altruistic attitude and work for free. The teacher needs to be engaged, but she also needs to be seen as a professional.

In this sense, it would be desirable for face-to-face teacher education courses to develop online practices so that future teachers would begin to incorporate the pace of online activities, and the differentiated strategies for participation that online teachers will need to develop, into their everyday experiences. We know that virtual learning environments like TIDIA-Ae and TelEduc are used in courses like the one offered at Unesp, Rio Claro, but we are not yet aware of courses that give priority to these questions or where they are emphasized in the pedagogical project of face-to-face courses for mathematics teachers. Until an evaluation of online mathematics teacher education projects has been carried out, we can at least affirm that teachers who have experienced online education will certainly know, at a minimum, how to use a virtual learning environment.

Our intention with the above discussion is far from solving various questions we have raised about teacher education throughout the book, but rather to contribute by making the link between specific research we have developed with teachers in online environments and public policies, which do not always reflect the voices of those who live the experiences being legislated. We hope that our contributions regarding the model of course based on interaction, the proposal for virtual communities of self-learning like the Virtual Center for Modeling, the concrete examples of how interactions in virtual learning environments take place, and the questions related to initial and continuing teacher education, serve to give continuity to debates on online distance education, based on research. Finally, we hope that the examples presented in this book, as well as the theoretical discussions, can shed light on other experiences in online distance education.

DISCUSSION QUESTIONS

In this section, we propose some questions that can serve to stimulate debate in face-to-face or virtual environments for those interested in online distance education. In some cases, the astute reader can find answers in the book, but in general, other references should be consulted to obtain a more complete framework for the problem, or even to cope with questions that were not addressed in the book. The questions are divided into groups based on themes.

POSSIBLE RELATIONS BETWEEN ONLINE DISTANCE EDUCATION AND TEACHER EDUCATION

- How should the teacher act in online distance education?
- Should there be practical internships in online distance education for teachers to learn how to deal with this educational modality?
- What are the advantages and disadvantages of using the expression "tutor" to designate the teacher who is often present in the classroom helping the teacher who is online?
- What does the law say about online teachers? What legislation would you propose to regulate various aspects of online distance education?
- As a teacher, would you prefer to take an online or face-to-face continuing education course? Why?
- What are the possible relations between the ubiquity of the Internet and pedagogical practices?

MODELS OF ONLINE COURSES

- Who would be interested in promoting models of courses that reproduce the television model, in which there is little interaction between the presenter and "viewers"?
- Does predominant use of one tool over another in a virtual learning environment, such as chat room or videoconference, modify the way participants in the course relate to each other?
- Should open access to all pages on the Internet be allowed in online courses? Why?
- Is it interesting for participants in courses, online or face-to-face, to

have responsibilities for leading debates in some of the classes? Why?

VIRTUAL PRACTICES IN EDUCATION

- What constitutes a virtual learning community?
- In what ways do virtual learning environments and their interfaces shape education?
- What are some possible roles of the Internet in the development of modeling projects?
- Do you believe a synergy exists between modeling and the Internet? Justify your answer.

RESEARCH METHODOLOGY IN ONLINE ENVIRONMENTS

- What does it mean to do research online?
- How does data collection take place online?
- Is triangulation possible online?
- Do data from online courses constitute documents? Justify your answer.
- What does it mean to say the Internet is a natural environment for the development of research?

REFERENCES

ACCIOLI, R.M. Robótica e as transformações geométricas: um estudo exploratório com alunos do ensino fundamental. 2005. Dissertação (Mestrado em Educação Matemática). Pontifícia Universidade Católica, São Paulo, 2005.

ALMEIDA, L.M.W.; DIAS, M.R. Um estudo sobre o uso da Modelagem Matemática como estratégia de ensino e aprendizagem. Bolema, ano 17, n. 22, p.19-35, 2004.

ALRØ, H.; SKOVSMOSE, O. Diálogo e aprendizagem em Educação Matemática. Tradução de FIGUEIREDO, O. Belo Horizonte: Autêntica, 2006.

ALVES-MAZZOTTI, A. O método nas Ciências Sociais. In: ALVES-MAZZOTTI, A. J.; GEWAMDSZNADJDER, F. O método nas ciências naturais e sociais: pesquisa quantitativa e qualitativa. 2ª reimp. 2ª ed. São Paulo: Pioneira, 2001. p. 107-188.

ARAÚJO, J.L. Cálculo, tecnologias e Modelagem Matemática: a discussão dos alunos. 2002. Tese (Doutorado em Educação Matemática) - Instituto de Geociências e Ciências Exatas, Universidade Estadual Paulista, Rio Claro, 2002.

ARAÚJO, J.L.; BORBA, M.C. Construindo pesquisas coletivamente em Educação Matemática. In: BORBA, M.C.; ARAUJO, J.L. (Org.). Pesquisa Qualitativa em Educação Matemática. Belo Horizonte: Autêntica, 2004. p. 25-45.

BAIRRAL, M.A. Desenvolvendo-se criticamente em Matemática: a formação continuada em ambientes virtualizados. In: FIORENTINI, D.; NACARATO, A.M. (Org.). Cultura, formação e desenvolvimento profissional de professores que ensinam Matemática: investigando e teorizando a partir da prática. São Paulo: Musa Editora; Campinas, SP: GEPFPM-PRAPEM-FE/UNICAMP, 2005. p. 49-67.

BAIRRAL, M.A. Compartilhando e construindo conhecimento matemático: análise do discurso nos chats. Bolema, ano 17, n. 22, p. 1-17, 2004.

BAIRRAL, M.A. Desarrollo profesional docente en Geometría: análisis de un proceso de Formación a Distancia. 2002. Tese (Doutorado em Didáctica de las Ciencias Experimentals i de las Matemáticas) – Universitat de Barcelona, Espanha, 2002.

BARBOSA, R.M. Descobrindo a Geometria Fractal para a sala de aula. Belo Horizonte: Autêntica, 2002.

BELLO, W.R. Possibilidades de Construção do Conhecimento em um Ambiente Telemático: análise de uma experiência de Matemática em EaD. 2004. Dissertação (Mestrado em Educação Matemática). Pontifícia Universidade Católica, São Paulo, 2004.

BELLONI, M.L. Educação a Distância. Campinas: Autores Associados, 2003.

BENEDETTI, F. Funções, software gráfico e coletivos penssante. 2003. Dissertação (Mestrado em Educação Matemática) – Instituto de Geociências e Ciências Exatas, Universidade Estadual Paulista, Rio Claro, 2003.

BICUDO, M.A.V. Pesquisa em Educação Matemática. Pró-Posições. Campinas, v. 4, n. 1[10], p. 16-23, 1993.

BICUDO, M.A.V. Fenomenologia: confrontos e avanços. São Paulo: Cortez, 2000.

BICUDO, M.A.V. Intersubjetividade e Educação. Didática. São Paulo, v. 15, p. 97-102, 1979.

BORBA, M.C. Diversidade de questões em formação de professores em Matemática. In: BORBA, M.C. (Org.). Tendências Internacionais em Formação de Professores de Matemática. Belo Horizonte: Autêntica, 2006, p. 9-26.

BICUDO, M.A.V. The transformation of mathematics in online courses. In: PSYCHOLOGY OF MATHEMATICS EDUCATION, 29., 2005, Australia. Proceedings... University of Melbourne, Austrália, 2005.

BICUDO, M.A.V. Dimensões da Educação Matemática a Distância. In: BICUDO, M.A.V.; BORBA, M. (Org.). Educação Matemática: pesquisa em movimento. São Paulo: Cortez, 2004, p.296-317.

BICUDO, M.A.V. O Computador é a solução: Mas qual é o Problema. In: SEVERINO, A.J.; FAZENDA. I.C.A. (Org.). Formação Docente: rupturas e possibilidades. Campinas: Papirus, 2002. p. 151-162.

BICUDO, M.A.V. Tecnologias Informáticas na Educação Matemática e Reorganização do Pensamento. In: BICUDO, M.A.V. (Ed.). Pesquisa em Educação Matemática: concepções e perspectivas. São Paulo: Editora UNESP, 1999a. p. 297-313.

BICUDO, M.A.V. Calculadoras gráficas e Educação Matemática. Rio de Janeiro: Universidade Santa Úrsula, 1999b. (Série reflexão em Educação Matemática, v. 6).

BICUDO, M.A.V. Informática trará mudanças na educação brasileira? Zetetiké, Campinas, v. 4, n. 6, jul./dez. p. 123-134, 1996.

BICUDO, M.A.V. Computadores, representações múltiplas e a construção de idéias matemáticas. Bolema, ano 9, especial 3, p. 83 – 101. 1994.

BICUDO, M.A.V. Students Understanding of Transformations of Functions Using Multi-Representational Software. 1993. Tese (Doutorado em Educação Matemática), Cornell University, Ithaca, 1993.

BICUDO, M.A.V. Um Estudo em Etnomatemática: sua incorporação na elaboração de uma proposta pedagógica para o núcleo-escola da vila Nogueira. 1987. 266f. Dissertação (Mestrado em Educação Matemática) – Instituto de Geociências e Ciências Exatas, Universidade Estadual Paulista, Rio Claro, 1987.

BORBA, M.C.; MALHEIROS, A.P.S. Diferentes formas de interação entre Internet e Modelagem: desenvolvimento de projetos e o CVM. In: BARBOSA, J.C.; CALDEIRA, A.D.; ARAÚJO, J.L. Modelagem Matemática na Educação Matemática Brasileira: Pesquisas e Práticas Educacionais. Recife: Sbem, 2007. p. 195-211. (Biblioteca do Educador Matemático). V.3.

BORBA, M.C.; VILLARREAL, M.E. Humans-with-Media and the Reorganization of Mathematical Thinking: Information and Communication Technologies, Modeling, Visualization and Experimentation. New York: Springer, 2005.

BORBA, M.C.; MALTEMPI, M.V.; MALHEIROS, A.P.S. Internet Avançada e Educação Matemática: novos desafios para o ensino e aprendizagem online. Renote, Porto Alegre, v. 3, n. 1, maio, 2005.

BORBA, M.C.; PENTEADO, M.G. Informática e Educação Matemática. Belo Horizonte: Autêntica, 2001.

BORBA, M.C.; SKOVSMOSE, O. A ideologia da certeza em Educação Matemática. In: SKOVSMOSE, O. Educação Matemática Crítica: a questão da democracia. Campinas: Papirus, 2001. p. 127-148.

BORBA, M.C.; MENEGHETTI, R.C.G.; HERMINI, H. A. Modelagem, Calculadora Gráfica e Interdisciplinaridade na sala de aula de um curso de Ciências Biológicas. In: FAINGUELERNT, E.K.; GOTTLIEB, F.C. (Org.). Calculadoras Gráficas e Educação Matemática. Rio de Janeiro: Art Bureau, 1999a. p. 75-94.

BORBA, M.C. Estabelecendo critérios para avaliação do uso de Modelagem em sala de aula: estudo de um caso em um curso de Ciências Biológicas. In: FAINGUELERNT, K.; GOTTLIEB, F.C. (Org.). Calculadoras gráficas e Educação Matemática. Rio de Janeiro: Art Bureau, 1999b. p. 95-113.

BRASIL. Ministério da Educação e Cultura. Secretaria Fundamental de Educação. Parâmetros Curriculares Nacionais: Matemática. Brasília: MEC/SEF, 1998.

CASTELLS, M. A Galáxia da internet: reflexões sobre internet, os negócios e a sociedade. Rio de Janeiro: Jorge Zahar, 2003.

REFERENCES

CIFUENTES, J.C. Uma via estética de acesso ao conhecimento matemático. Boletim GEPEM, Rio de Janeiro, n. 46, p. 55-72, jan./jun., 2005.

DENZIN, N.K; LINCOLN, Y.S. The discipline and practice of qualitative research, In: DENZIN, N.K. Handbook of qualitative research. 2. ed. Londres: Sage, 2000.

DINIZ, L.N. O Papel das Tecnologias da Informação e Comunicação nos Projetos de Modelagem Matemática. 2007. Dissertação (Mestrado em Educação Matemática) – Instituto de Geociências e Ciências Exatas, Universidade Estadual Paulista, Rio Claro, 2007.

FIORENTINI, D. Pesquisar práticas colaborativas ou pesquisar colaborativamente? In: BORBA, M.C.; ARAUJO, J.L. (Org.). Pesquisa Qualitativa em Educação Matemática. Belo Horizonte: Autêntica, 2004, p. 47-76.

FONSECA, M.C.F.R.; LOPES, M.P.; BARBOSA, M.G.G.; GOMES, M.L.M.; DAYRELL, M.M.M.S.S. O ensino da geometria na escola fundamental: três questões para a formação do professor dos ciclos iniciais. Belo Horizonte: Autêntica, 2001.

FRAGALE FILHO, R. O contexto legislativo da Educação a Distância. In: FRAGALE FILHO, R. (Org.). Educação a distância: análise dos parâmetros legais e normativos. Rio de Janeiro: DP&A, 2003. p. 13-26.

FERREIRA, A.C.; MIORIM, M.A. O grupo de trabalho em educação matemática: análise de um processo vivido. In: SEMINÁRIO INTERNACIONAL DE PESQUISA EM EDUCAÇÃO MATEMÁTICA, 2., Santos. Anais... Santos, SP, 2003. 1CD-ROM.

FREIRE, P. Pedagogia do oprimido. 45. ed. Rio de Janeiro: Paz e Terra, 2005.

GARNICA, A.V.M. Fascínio da técnica, declínio da crítica: um estudo sobre a prova rigorosa na formação do professor de Matemática. 1995. Tese (Doutorado em Educação Matemática) – Instituto de Geociências e Ciências Exatas, Universidade Estadual Paulista, Rio Claro, 1995.

GOLDENBERG, M. A arte de pesquisar: como fazer pesquisa qualitativa em Ciências Sociais. 3.ed. Rio de Janeiro: Record, 1999.

GONZALEZ, M. Fundamentos da tutoria em Educação a Distância. São Paulo: Avercamp, 2005.

GRACIAS, T.A.S. A Reorganização do pensamento em um curso a distância sobre Tendências em Educação Matemática. 2003. Tese (Doutorado em Educação Matemática) – Instituto de Geociências e Ciências Exatas, Universidade Estadual Paulista, Rio Claro, 2003.

GUÉRIOS, E. Espaços intersticiais na formação docente: indicativos para a formação continuada de professores que ensinam Matemática. In: FIORENTINI, D.; NACARATO, A.M. (Org.). Cultura, formação e desenvolvimento profissional de professores que ensinam Matemática: investigando e teorizando a partir da prática. São Paulo: Musa Editora; Campinas, SP: GEPFPM-PRAPEM-FE/UNICAMP, 2005. p.128-151.

HARGREAVES, A. O ensino como profissão paradoxal. Pátio. Porto Alegre, ano 4, n. 16, fev./abr., 2001.

IMENES, L.M.P.; LELLIS, M. Matemática. São Paulo: Scipione, 1997.

JACOBINI , O.R. A Modelagem Matemática como instrumento de ação política na sala de aula. 2004. Tese (Doutorado em Educação Matemática) – Instituto de Geociências e Ciências Exatas, Universidade Estadual Paulista, Rio Claro, 2004.

MACHADO JÚNIOR, A.G.; SANTO, A.O.E.; SILVA, F.H.S. O ambiente de Modelagem Matemática e a Aprendizagem dos alunos: relatos de experiência. In: SEMINÁRIO INTERNACIONAL DE PESQUISA EM EDUCAÇÃO MATEMÁTICA, 3., Águas de Lindóia. Anais... Águas de Lindóia, SP, 2006. 1CD-ROM.

KENSKI, V.M. Tecnologias e ensino presencial e a distância. Campinas: Papirus, 2003.

LABORDE, C. Relationships between the spatial and theoretical in geometry: the role of computer dynamic representations in problem solving. In: INSLEY, D.; JOHNSON, D.C. (Ed.). Information and communications technologies in school mathematics. Grenoble: Champman and Hall, 1998.

LÉVY, P. Cibercultura. Rio de Janeiro: Editora 34, 1. reimp., 1999.

LÉVY, P. As tecnologias da inteligência: o futuro do pensamento na era da informática. Rio de Janeiro: Editora 34, 1993.

LIMA, E. CARVALHO, P.C.P.; WAGNER, E.; MORGADO, A.C. A Matemática do ensino médio. Coleção do Professor de Matemática. v. 2. Rio de Janeiro: Sociedade Brasileira de Matemática, 1999.

LINCOLN, Y.S.; GUBA, E. G. Naturalistic Inquiry. Califórnia: Sage, 1985.

LOBO, F.S. Educação a distância: regulamentação. Brasília: Plano, 2000.

LOPES, A. Avaliação em Educação Matemática a Distância: uma experiência de Geometria no ensino médio. 2004. Dissertação (Mestrado em Educação Matemática). Universidade Pontifícia Católica, São Paulo, 2004.

LOURENÇO, M.L. A demonstração com informática aplicada à Educação. Bolema, ano 15, n.18, p.100-111, 2002.

MACHADO, N.J. Matemática e língua materna: análise de uma impregnação mútua. São Paulo: Cortez, 2001.

MAIA, C. Guia brasileiro de educação a distância (2002/2003). São Paulo: Esfera, 2002.

MALHEIROS, A.P.S. Contextualizando o design emergente numa pesquisa sobre Modelagem Matemática e Educação a Distância. In: ENCONTRO BRASILEIRO DE ESTUDANTES DE PÓS-GRADUAÇÃO EM EDUCAÇÃO MATEMÁTICA, 10. Belo Horizonte. Anais... Belo Horizonte: Universidade Federal de Minas Gerais, Faculdade de Educação, 2006.

MALHEIROS, A.P.S. A produção matemática dos alunos em ambiente de modelagem. Dissertação. 2004. (Mestrado em Educação Matemática) – Instituto de Geociências e Ciências Exatas, Universidade Estadual Paulista, Rio Claro, 2004.

MARTINS, J.; BICUDO, M.A.V. A pesquisa qualitativa em Psicologia: fundamentos e recursos básicos. 5. ed. São Paulo: Centauro, 2005.

MISKULIN, R.G.S. et al. Pesquisas sobre trabalho colaborativo na formação de professores de matemática: um olhar sobre a produção do PRAPEM/UNICAMP. In: FIORENTINI, D.; NACARATO, A.M. (Org.). Cultura, formação e desenvolvimento profissional de professores que ensinam Matemática: investigando e teorizando a partir da prática. São Paulo: Musa Editora; Campinas: GEPFPM-PRAPEM -FE/UNICAMP, 2005.

MORAN, J.M.M. O que é educação a distância. 2002. Disponível em: <http://www.eca.usp.br/prof/moran/dist.htm>. Acesso em: 12 jan. 2006.

NACARATO, A.M. A escola como lócus de formação e de aprendizagem: possibilidades e riscos de colaboração. In: FIORENTINI, D.; NACARATO, A.M. (Org.). Cultura, formação e desenvolvimento profissional de professores que ensinam Matemática: investigando e teorizando a partir da prática. São Paulo: Musa Editora; Campinas, SP: GEPFPM-PRAPEM-FE/UNICAMP, 2005.

OLIVERO, F.; ARZARELLO, F.; MICHELETTI, C.; ROBUTTI, O. Dragging in Cabri and modalities of transition from conjectures to proofs in geometry. In: PSYCHOLOGY OF MATHEMATICS EDUCATION, 22., Stellenbosh, South Africa. Proceedings... Stellenbosh, South Africa, 1998.

PALLOFF, M.R.; PRATT, K. Construindo comunidades de aprendizagem no ciberespaço: estratégias eficientes para a sala de aula online. Porto Alegre: Artmed, 2002.

PENTEADO, M.G. Computer-based learning environments: risks and uncertainties for teacher. Ways of Knowing Journal, v. 1, 2001.

PENTEADO, M.; BORBA, C.M. (Org.). A informática em ação: formação de professores, pesquisa e extensão. São Paulo: Olho D'Água, 2000.

PEREZ, G.; COSTA, G.L.M.; VIEL, S.R. Desenvolvimento profissional e prática reflexiva. Bolema, ano 15, n. 17, p. 59-70, 2002.

PETERS, O. A educação a distância em transição. São Leopoldo: Unisinos, 2002.

PRADO, M.E.B.; ALMEIDA, M.E.B.P. Redesenhando estratégias na própria ação: formação do professor a distância em ambiente digital. In: VALENTE, J.A.; PRADO, M.E.B.B.; ALMEIDA, M.E.B. Educação a distância via internet. São Paulo: Avercamp, 2003.

ROSA, M. ; MALTEMPI, M.V . A avaliação vista sob o aspecto da educação a distância. Ensaio – Avaliação e Políticas Públicas em Educação, v.14, p. 57-75, 2006.

SACRAMENTO, M.C.A.F. Docência online: rupturas e possibilidades para a prática educativa. 2006. Dissertação (Mestrado em Educação e Contemporaneidade). Universidade Estadual da Bahia, Salvador, 2006.

SANTOS, S.C. A Produção Matemática em um Ambiente Virtual de Aprendizagem: o caso da geometria Euclidiana Espacial. 2006. Dissertação (Mestrado em Educação Matemática) – Instituto de Geociências e Ciências Exatas, Universidade Estadual Paulista, Rio Claro, 2006.

SAVIANI, D. Educação: do senso comum à consciência filosófica. São Paulo: Cortez, 1985.

SCUCUGLIA, R. A investigação do teorema Fundamental do Cálculo com calculadoras gráficas. 2006. Dissertação (Mestrado em Educação Matemática) – Instituto de Geociências e Ciências Exatas, Universidade Estadual Paulista, Rio Claro, 2006.

SILVA, M. EAD online, cibercultura e interatividade. In: ALVES, L.; NOVA, C. (Org.). Educação a Distância: uma nova concepção de aprendizado e interatividade. São Paulo: Futura, 2003a. p. 51-73.

SILVA, M. Apresentação. In: SILVA, M. (Org.). Educação online. São Paulo: Loyola, 2003b. p.11-20.

TIKHOMIROV, O.K. The Psychological consequences of computerization. In: WERTTSCH, J.V. (Ed.). The Concept of Activity in Soviet Psychology. New York: M. E. Sharpe, 1981.

TORRES, P.L. Laboratório online de aprendizagem: uma proposta crítica de aprendizagem colaborativa para a educação. Tubarão: Editora Unisul, 2004.

TOSCHI, M.S.; RODRIGUES, M. E. C. Infovias e educação. Educação e Pesquisa. v. 29, n. 2, p. 313-326, dez. 2003.

VALENTE, J.A. Criando ambientes de aprendizagem via rede telemática:

experiências na formação de professores para o uso da informática na educação. In: VALENTE, J.A. (Org.). Formação de educadores para o uso da informática na escola. Campinas: UNICAMP/NIED, 2003a.

VALENTE, J.A. Cursos de especialização em desenvolvimento de projetos pedagógicos com o uso das novas tecnologias: descrição e fundamentos. In: VALENTE, J.A.; PRADO, M.E.B.B.; ALMEIDA, M.E.B. Educação a distância via internet. São Paulo: Avercamp, 2003b.

VIANNEY, J.; TORRES, P.; SILVA, E. A universidade virtual no Brasil. Tubarão: Editora Unisul, 2003.

VILLARREAL, M.E. O pensamento matemático de estudantes universitários de cálculo e tecnologias informáticas. 1999. Tese (Doutorado em Educação Matemática) – Instituto de Geociências e Ciências Exatas, Universidade Estadual Paulista, Rio Claro, 1999.

ZIMMERMANN, W.; CUNNINGHAM, S. Editors' Introduction: What is Mathematical Visualization? In: *Visualization in teaching and learning Mathematics*, W. Zimmermann and S. Cunningham, eds., Mathematical Association of America, Washington, DC, pp.1-8. 1991.

ZULATTO, R.B.A. A natureza da aprendizagem matemática em um ambiente online de formação continuada de professores. 2007. Tese (Doutorado em Educação Matemática) – Instituto de Geociências e Ciências Exatas, Universidade Estadual Paulista, Rio Claro, 2007.

ZULATTO, R.B.A.; BORBA, M.C. Diferentes mídias, diferentes tipos de trabalhos coletivos em cursos de formação continuada de professores a distância: pode me passar a caneta, por favor? In: SEMINÁRIO INTERNACIONAL DE PESQUISA EM EDUCAÇÃO MATEMÁTICA, 3., Águas de Lindóia, SP, Anais... p. 41-56. 2006.

FOOTNOTES

Introduction

[1] Details can be found at:
http://www.anatel.gov.br/index.asp?link=/biblioteca/editais/fust/default.htm

Chapter I

[1] Grupo de Pesquisa em Informática, outras Mídias e Educação Matemática (Research Group in Computers, Other Media, and Mathematics Education),
http://www.rc.unesp.br/igce/pgem/gpimem.html.

[2] PNE – Plano Nacional de Educação (National Education Plan).

[3] In this same sense, other authors make similar classifications, such as Peters (2002), who classifies these paradigms as follows: www (myself-alone), e-mail (one-to-one), BBS (one-to-many), and videoconference (many-to-many).

Chapter II

[1] We use this term when the participants are teachers, and are students in the context of the courses.

[2] Universidade Estadual Paulista "Júlio de Mesquita Filho" (São Paulo State University).

[3] For more details, consult Borba (2004; 2005), Borba and Villarreal (2005), Malheiros, (2006), Rosa and Maltempi (2006), Santos (2006), and Zulatto (2007).

[4] To avoid repetition, we will also use "Trends" to refer to the Trends in Mathematics Education courses.

[5] http://teleduc.nied.unicamp.br/teleduc/.

[6] Environment developed by a consortium of research groups, including GPIMEM, financed by the São Paulo State Research Foundation (Fundação de Amparo à Pesquisa do Estado de São Paulo – FAPESP), entitled Information Technologies in the Development of Advanced Internet – Electronic Learning. For more information: http://tidia-ae.incubadora.fapesp.br/portal.

[7] Dynamic Geometry Software developed by Viggo Sadolin (The Royal Danish of Education Studies, Kopenhagen, Denmark) and translated into Portuguese by Miriam Godoy Penteado and Marcelo de Carvalho Borba, UNESP, Rio Claro. Editora da UNESP, 2001. http://www.rc.unesp.br/igce/matematica/tricks/.

[8] For more information and to download, access: http://math.exeter.edu/rparris/winplot.html.

[9] Since it is not our objective to investigate specific questions related to writing in chat, some errors were corrected to avoid confusing the reader.

[10] Marcelo Badin, a high school mathematics teacher in Rio Claro, São Paulo, Brazil, who was a Masters student in the Graduate Program in Mathematics Education, UNESP, Rio Claro, was invited to participate due to his familiarity with the theme in debate, and because of his interest in discussing mathematics via distance. In other versions of the course, we had other invited guests in an effort to create an online distance education culture.

[11] For additional information and to download, see http://math.exeter.edu/rparris/wingeom.html.

[12] Activity adapted by Silvana Claudia Santos from the work of Lima et al. (1999).

Chapter III

[1] Plataform CentraOne, available for participants at: http://www.conferencia.org.br.

[2] Image captured by a webcam which could belong to the professors or the teacher-students.

[3] There were people connected at distant locations whose connection would become slow and possibly be interrupted if the image were made available on the site.

[4] This activity was adapted from the textbook used by the Bradesco Foundation for the elementary grade levels. (IMENES; LELLIS, 1997).

Chapter IV

[1] This trend will be presented in Chapter V.

[2] Human-Computer Interection, See more details at http://pt.wikipedia.org/wiki/Intera%C3%A7%C3%A3o_homem-computador.

Chapter V

[1] Instant messaging for the Web. http://get.live.com/messenger/overview.

[2] Online community that connects people through a network http://www.orkut.com.

[3] Environment developed by a consortium of research groups, including GPIMEM, financed by the São Paulo State Research Foundation (Fundação de Amparo à Pesquisa do Estado de São Paulo – FAPESP), entitled Information Technologies in the Development of Advanced Internet – Electronic Learning. For more information: http://tidia-ae.incubadora.fapesp.br/portal. Because it is associated with a collaborative research project, the environment is undergoing constant modification, for example, insertion of new tools as they are developed.

[4] Those interested in accessing the VCM can send an e-mail to cvm@rc.unesp.br and request to sign up.

[5] More details at http://www.csus.edu/indiv/o/oreyd/trilha/op.trilha.index.htm.

[6] State University of Pará, http://www2.uepa.br/uepa_site/.

[7] Doctoral dissertation of Ana Paula dos Santos Malheiros, 2008, Graduate Program in Mathematics Education, São Paulo State University (UNESP), Rio Claro campus.

[8] http://www.skype.com/.

[9] http://pt.wikipedia.org/.

Chapter VI

[1] http://www.educacional.com.br/.

[2] To sign up, access http://listas.rc.unesp.br/mailman/listinfo/sbem-l and fill out the electronic form, including your e-mail address.

[3] http://www.edu.uwo.ca/dmp/.

[4] http://mecsrv04.mec.gov.br/sef/fundeb/.

LaVergne, TN USA
30 July 2010
191539LV00001B/7/P